MW00596511

In Northern Maine there stands a mountain named Katahdin.
On its summit, a sign marks the northern terminus
of the Appalachian Trail.
The name means "The Greatest Mountain."

Sole Searching on the Appalachian Trail

Sam "Sam I Am" Ducharme

Rose Publishing

ISBN: 978-1-7329064-0-2

Designed by: Cameron Taylor
Text set in Goudy Old Style
Printed in the United States of America
Rose Publishing 2017

Dedication

John and Penny

Acknowledgement

Special thanks to Cameron Taylor who kept this project moving forward, and Priscilla Colwell for all her help and encouragement. I would also like to thank Red Hot for allowing me to be a part of his life-long dream.

Table of Contents

"There are three things: to walk, to see, and to see what you see."

Benton MacKaye
Creator of the Appalachian Trail

Introduction

Okay, so I thru-hiked the Appalachian Trail. Thousands of people have done it. It's not like I am Lewis or Clark; I didn't discover anything. All I did was follow a well-used trail. There are about 165,000 white blazes painted on trees and rocks ensuring I didn't get lost. I didn't even need a compass, map or GPS. When I put it this way, it doesn't even seem like a feat at all. For me, however, next to raising a couple of boys to adulthood, it was the hardest thing I ever did.

The first thing many of us newly-accomplished "thru-hikers" want to do is rush home, wash the trail off, eat some real food and write a book. The truth of the matter is that we all could write a book and no two would be the same. We all have our own stories. Our reasons differ for wanting to go. We have different styles, hiking speeds, gear and plans. We also leave the trail with our own results. Some stay connected to the trail forever; others can take the experience with them and never return. No thru-hiker will argue that the trail will ever leave them though, that experience will stay with us forever.

This isn't a "How-to," or a gear guide on "What you need to hike the AT." This is one story of a 49-year-old man from New England who, on his own, went out and bought a backpack and a plane ticket to Atlanta, and started walking home. I won't be killing you with gear specs, historical facts or tons of geological or botanical terms. I'm not that smart. I will share my experiences regarding this awesome journey in a down to earth, light and happy tone – the way I live every day.

I'm getting ahead of myself. You bought a book that you already know the ending to. That is exactly what I thought when I started out. Well, it was one of two possibilities. Finish as a thru-hiker, or fail. In the beginning neither outcome was that important, I just thought it would be neat to try. Slowly, however, this hike became a journey. A journey I intended to conclude by standing on Katahdin, the finish line. So to speak.

The odds of successfully completing a thru-hike are stacked against anyone. We are talking about hiking over two thousand miles along the Appalachian Mountain range through three seasons. It is estimated that it will require around five million steps to accomplish. When you think that all five million steps must happen without resulting in a fall that will render you unable to finish, each and every one – over mountains, slippery roots and steep descents – it's impossible to figure the odds against you. Now, place a heavy pack on the back of a clumsy guy who never back-packed before, and my odds of finishing were exponentially lower. Those of you who have backpacked know it's not about the destination; it's the in-between that you remember. When I started I thought you just had to know how to walk. The rest I learned along the way. Those were hard lessons.

With no further ado, let me take you on a little hike; a hike that takes us through fourteen states, 2,189.2 miles, through three seasons and almost six months. Before we head out though, there are some things you should know about the Appalachian Trail.

The Trail

The Appalachian Trail, known too many and henceforth the AT, is an old and long trail. It isn't a historical trail. Native Americans didn't use it to travel from wintering grounds to summer grounds. John Adams didn't use it to travel to meetings in Virginia during the birth of our nation. Nope. The AT is a hiking trail. In fact, it is many trails connected to make one continuous trail. The concept was born in 1921 by Benton MacKaye who claimed to have come up with the idea while sitting in a tree in Vermont. It was officially finished in 1937. The trail was part of a growing popularity of hiking to escape the stress of urban life. (I suppose the crash of the Hindenburg and the loss of Amelia Earhart would actually drive some people to seek solitude in the forest!)

The AT is strenuous. When you think of hiking a distance almost as long as walking from Washington, D.C., to Las Vegas, it seems crazy. But when you throw 300 mountains in between, it becomes ludicrous! The highest point of the trail is located in the Great Smokey National Park and is 6,643 feet. The lowest elevation is 124 feet above sea level in Bear Mountain State Park in New York. Yes, there is a lot of up and down. Thru-hikers – people who hike the trail in its entirety within one year – will climb and descend the equivalent to climbing and descending Mt. Everest from sea level 16 times! You'd think all that climbing would be rough on your body. It is. Most long-distance hikers will tell you, the down hills are the worst. Gravity is definitely on your side, but when you are carrying extra weight, taking unnatural steps of different sizes and angles, and factor in fatigue and traction – or lack of traction – the descents are worse. Take my word for it. I learned enough knee terminology to apply for a trainer position for the Boston Red Sox!

Thru-hiking is an outdoor activity. I'm stating the obvious, right? Who doesn't love camping? It's fun, especially when you can use a restroom and a hot shower at the campground or in the RV. After about a week on the trail it becomes very clear that you now live outdoors. This "realization stage" is where the highest percentage of thru-hike attempts fail.

There are 262 shelters between Springer Mountain in Georgia and Katahdin, Maine. A shelter, or lean-to as they are called in Maine, is a three-sided structure with a floor or platform for sleeping. Many hikers find these cute, shed-like buildings more convenient than setting up a tent every night. Many who tent-camp most of the time, favor the shelters during bad weather. Despite the weather, good, bad, cold or hot, you are still living outdoors. Some hikers don't even carry a tent, opting to shave the weight from their pack, and sleep in shelters exclusively. You can stay moderately dry, even out of the wind when it is not blowing straight in, and some shelters even look like a cabin, but you are still outdoors. The mosquitoes will remind you lest you forget.

Lots of women hike the AT. According to the Appalachian Trail Conservancy (ATC), 25% of thru-hikers are women. There is nothing quite like the feeling you get when you are folded over on a climb, gasping for breath, and a petite woman sails on by humming a cute little number from Julie Andrews. (Guys, before you decide to skip your next semester at college and go meet a woman on the AT, you better get in shape!)

The AT is a popular place. When I hiked, over 15,000 people had completed the whole trail. That number, according to the ATC, includes those hikers who completed it over a number of years.

Although they are not thru-hikers, they are "2000 Milers." This is a most impressive distinction in its own right. Here is why: Those hikers are referred to as "Section-Hikers," Section-hikers who become 2000 Milers, give up their vacation time and drive all over the East Coast to trail heads, to chip away the sections. Over time, sometimes a lifetime, they complete the whole trail. That means they have to grind through the conditioning phase of long-distance backpacking EVERY time out! A thru-hiker spends the first few weeks slowly getting into shape and hikes the majority of the trail in that condition. Section-hikers have to recondition themselves every trip out! Often, by the time their legs get in trail shape, they are completing their section! My hat is off to all you section-hikers. The mere thought of reliving that first month of torture makes me shudder!

In 2015, 3,064 people attempted a thru-hike. Less than a thousand finished. Although that is a pretty high percentage of finishers, it is less than one half of one percent of the total amount of hikers that used the trail! It is estimated that three million people hiked a portion of the trail that year. It has become a busy place! Just ask any hiker who got up at 3 a.m. to hike up to McAfee Knob for a picture of the sunrise, only to find 40 people already there for the same reason!

You can still find solitude. Because most hikers tend to hike the same speed, you can find yourself hiking for hours alone. Obviously, the more remote you are, the better your chances are to find this solitude. Times like these, when you find yourself lonely or insecure, it is good to have a way to connect to other hikers. I have developed a fail proof way of doing just that: I just stop and take a pee. Someone is sure to come hiking down the trail at that moment.

Why?

It is the first question asked when people find out I thru-hiked the Appalachian Trail. Everyone has their own reason. Some like Cheryl Strayed, who hiked the Pacific Crest Trail and was portrayed by Reese Witherspoon in Wild, set out to deal with the loss of her mother, depression, drug abuse and a failed marriage. Others find themselves looking for adventure, and solitude. I met several military Vets who set out for various reasons, most trying to readjust to civilian life following a tour of duty in the Middle East. Over half of the thru-hikers are in their twenties, taking a break between college and a career. They're young adults who aren't yet committed to a family or career, and can schedule something that requires no schedule. Others are fulfilling a lifelong dream that they planned for years. They saved, studied and sacrificed for this trip. For every hiker there is their own personal "why." In order to understand my "why" maybe you need to get to know me a little.

When I decided to hike the AT I was 49 years old, retired from the State of Connecticut Department of Correction with two grown boys serving in the United States Air Force. Having been a canine officer, my canine partner and best friend Stix, had recently passed and I found myself in the unfamiliar position of being responsibility free.

Having worked as an officer in the prison system for twenty years, I had become worn down by the unique characteristics of that career. Let's face it; a prison is a negative environment. The inmates are untrustworthy, tiresome, needy and dangerous. Being a K-9 officer is similar to being a firefighter. The training is hard, you have a lot of responsibilities, and it is a ticket to the front of the line when things get rough. Mostly though, when you get called, things get hectic fast.

I managed to keep my usual upbeat attitude throughout my career and only those closest to me could see the subtle changes that years in that environment was making on me. Slowly, I became less patient of the inmates, staff and the overall negativity that eats away at you inside the walls and razor wire. It gets to us all, eventually. I was much older than when I started; wise to the criminal element, I constantly stereotyped people, and trusted no one. Working inside the prisons, changes the way you live outside the prisons. I retired with a smile, happy to be healthy, proud of a job well done, and grateful for a few breaks I got along the way. But I was worn out.

I know, that doesn't fully tell you the "why." If I was worn out, it doesn't seem logical to hike over two thousand miles, right? Well, I had a connection to the trail; I am from New England. More specifically, I have property in Maine and when I walk out of my garage, I look right at Katahdin, the northern terminus of the AT.

I'll back up a little. I am an avid outdoorsman. I love to hunt and fish and proudly raised my boys outdoors doing the things country boys do. One of those things was spending a lot of time in Maine where there is a lot of room to do that. We fished the rivers and lakes, swam in the waterfalls, explored the north woods, and rode our four wheelers so far we would arrive back on fuel reserve. I'm sure that lifestyle is why I was able to manage a stressful career, as well as raise two patriotic American Airmen. One summer, while in Maine, we climbed Katahdin. It was late August, and when we got to the summit we met a small group of skinny, stinky people who looked homeless. They were obviously thrilled with their feat and visibly emotional. What stuck with me the most was how they seemed to worship the summit sign. They were taking pictures together and just standing there touching it. It wasn't particularly nice out; there were low threatening clouds. Storms were brewing and it seemed like heading down the mountain was a good idea. For these people though, they didn't even seem to notice. Hey, I was pretty tired from the climb myself, but I didn't think it was such a big deal, so I inquired.

Sitting on the jagged rocks 5,269 feet above sea level, I listened to six hikers tell me about their thru-hike from Georgia that took them through 14 states on the Appalachian Trail. It was fascinating. They told funny stories, scary stories of treacherous weather, camping stories, and sad stories of fellow hikers who had to drop out. I was amazed. After a while, and with the storm approaching fast, we said our goodbyes with fist bumps and congratulations until thunder scattered us like mice. As I was hunkered under a rock covered with a poncho waiting out what developed into a "wickid pissah" (as we like to say in New England) storm, I still couldn't fathom the journey those hikers had accomplished! Hiking through a hundred mile wilderness! That alone blew my mind, never mind the other 2,070 miles! I thought... "I'd like to do that someday." The seed was planted.

Following my retirement and seeing my boys off to the Air Force, I began thinking that a thru-hike was a cool idea. I originally thought I'd plan for a year, do research, gather gear and physically train. But looking ahead I decided that going sooner than later was better. So in February I decided I'd go in March. Up to this point I'd led an exciting life. I'd found myself in a prison yard surrounded by rioting inmates, jumped out of airplanes, and swam across a lake in a panic because I thought my son was drowning on the other side. I've rafted whitewater in Colorado, shot bear with my bow and raised two boys to adulthood. It's how I live. Experts call it a dynamic type A personality. I call it living. Regardless what it's called, the thought of a few months in the wilderness seemed like a peaceful change of pace and I was ready. As an avid hunter, I figured all those hours spent in the woods with a gun and bow, dealing with the elements, navigation and the sheer comfort of being outdoors made a thru-hike a natural fit with my lifestyle. That was my "WHY."

I had a month before I would leave so I had some work to do.

Pre-Trip

My clock was ticking and I figured that if I was going to complete this hike by October, I had better give myself plenty of time to do it. Baxter State Park in Maine, the northern terminus of the AT and home to Katahdin, closes in mid-October, so I planned on a March 15 start date. I know some hikers manage to winter climb that mountain, but I didn't want to. That meant I had to get my ducks in a row fast! Did I mention I had never backpacked before? Sure, a hike here and a hike there, but other than a few adventurous day-hikes with my kids and lugging a tree stand and rifle out to the woods, I never backpacked. I never even owned a backpack! I love taking my hammock out to deer camp and sleeping outside. I did that a lot, but I never had to live in it. Research was in order.

Like all modern day researchers, I booted up the computer and clicked on YouTube. I learned about the trail, how to get supplies, the gear I would need, shoes and clothes, how to cook, and how to get to Springer Mountain, Georgia, the southern terminus. I was watching YouTubers all night long for a month. To be sure I could find all that I needed; I even located a store that I had never heard of called REI.

Those REI folks were so nice. When I told them I was planning to thru-hike the Appalachian Trail and had no prior hiking experience, they closed down a whole section of the store to help me find gear. I think they even called in overtime. They had me trying on the latest and greatest footwear, hiking up and down their stairs, around the kayaks and through the bike section. I wasn't sure but I thought I heard them chuckle a couple times, but who could blame them? The new hi-tech shorts I needed with the zip-off legs looked funny when there was four feet of snow outside.

I kept asking them for a bag but no one seemed to know what I was talking about. I pointed them out between the tents and the GoPros, and apparently they refer to them as packs. Who knew? They found a great big one with long straps to fit around my belly and off I went again, marching around the store with a pack filled with bags of sand.

After several laps, another specialist escorted me to the "sleep system" area where I was startled to hear my old sleeping bag was not fit for a thru-hike. I needed special goose down that was waterproof. I thought all goose feathers were waterproof. Wasn't that why they are called waterfowl? I didn't want to argue, she must have been a biologist with knowledge of the exact bird that had the feathers I needed, so I threw a new "sleep system" into my "pack."

The next specialist was real helpful. He May have saved my life because I didn't see the YouTube video on little stuff. He must have had a degree in containers. He loaded me up with containers for my phone, my charger, tooth brush, soap, bags for my clothes and food, even a bag to smoosh my "new wave down feathered" sleeping system. I was starting to feel like a real hiker.

Did you know REI even has a specialist for cook systems? Well they do. Come to find out I didn't need her though; I was going to make a stove out of a beer can like I saw on YouTube. She did talk me into a small titanium cup though. Throw it in the pack. Now, try to conceive this: For twenty years I watched inmates eat their chow with small plastic sporks. Now this "cook system specialist" was trying to convince me that I needed to pay twenty bucks for a titanium spork! Yup, throw it in the pack.

According to the clothing specialist, my extensive collection of Harley Davidson T-shirts and sweatshirts don't have the correct "properties" to take on this hike. I asked if Cabala's would work. Nope. L.L. Bean? Nope. Now I was getting self-conscious. I was heading into the great outdoors without camo on, it just didn't seem right.

I was learning a lot. Not only were geese evolving, but sheep were getting smart, too. I got Smartwool shirts, Smartwool socks, even Smartwool underwear! I was a little worried about the underwear though, if they were anything like the mittens my mom knitted for me, it was going to be uncomfortable. As nice as the clothing specialist was, I had to draw the line at the poofy. I explained that I just worked in a manly environment for twenty years and I couldn't wear anything called a poofy! He explained that it was a lightweight jacket. I asked him if we could just call it what it was. I couldn't believe how light it was. I removed my handgun and stuffed the whole "lightweight jacket" in my holster! That's when he told me I should leave my firearm at home with my camo sweatshirts. I thought he was un-American, come to find out he was referring to the extra weight. The jacket and new space-age raincoat went into the pack, too.

It was getting late and I told the store manager I was sorry for keeping all his specialists late. He assured me it was okay as I headed to the register with all my new hiking gear. I felt like I was graduating high school again because all the specialists were lined up shaking my hand and wishing me luck. They each had something I somehow overlooked. The "backpack specialist" had a neat cover for my pack, the "cook system specialist" had a water filtration system, some other specialist had a water bottle, and I almost forgot my wilderness first aid kit. (I hadn't been around this many specialists since my last colonoscopy!)

I guess it was the bike specialist because I hadn't met him yet and there isn't much work for a bike specialist in Connecticut in February. He was nice enough to help me carry all this new gear to my truck. As I left I heard everyone cheering. They must have been having a late Christmas party or something. All I knew was – I was ready.

Returning home with my debit card still smoking, I couldn't wait to organize my pack. I removed the packaging and stuffed everything in. Luckily I already owned a hammock and tarp so I saved a few bucks there. I could hardly wait to set my hammock up in the yard and test out my new sleeping bag. It took me a while but I dug a spot between two trees and hung my hammock. You could barely see it with the snow piles. (I told you we had a lot of snow.) My new bag was rated to 15 degrees, but I learned that my Kindle wasn't. Good to know. I slept like a baby dreaming of Georgia peaches and chirping birds, but my neighbors thought I was nuts.

Any good AT researcher worth his weight in salt knows you have to prepare food boxes. These are boxes of food to be sent to you when you need to resupply. My buddy Mark was going to handle the shipping, all I had to do was set up a few boxes and tell him where to ship them. I learned that post offices along the trail will hold the boxes until the hikers pick them up. So off to the grocery store I went.

I filled my cart with tuna packs, oatmeal, peanut butter, Nutella, tortillas, coffee packs, energy bars and every Cliff Bar I could get my hands on. The cashier gave me a scowl as I placed all that on the belt along with dozens of Knorr Rice Sides and Ramen noodles. I should have waited to buy peanut M&Ms though; I ate them all before I left for Georgia. I spent the next couple days sorting it all out and preparing ten boxes.

With my gear packed and tested, food boxes delivered to Mark, and my plane ticket booked, I still wasn't ready to leave. I pride myself in living the simple life but there were still a couple loose ends I needed to tend to. I had to suspend my interweb, satellite TV, OnStar, XM radio; arrange my bills for auto pay; notify my bank; hold my mail; arrange my snow plowing, lawn care, and paper delivery. I asked Bobcat Bob, my nearest buddy, to swing by a couple times a week to check on the house. "Feel free to shoot some pool and switch the lights around to make it look like there's some life in the place while I'm away." He sure did a good job, too. When I returned there were cases of empty beer bottles on the porch and a bunch of new stains on the poker table. (A good friend like that is hard to find.)

I had one last thing to do which I was kind of dreading; tell the new boss. After a few months of retirement I started working for the local Chevy garage turning wrenches. I like that type of work, the garage banter was fun and the extra money was nice. I had been working there over a year and now I had to face my boss with my plans to leave. Not that he was scary or mean, just the opposite. He was patient, flexible with my schedule and put up with my zest for life (you don't always know how loud you sing when you are wearing ear protection). He was disappointed with the news but was supportive. In fact he told me to lock up my toolbox and leave it in my bay; my job would be waiting for me when I returned. That is a good company to work for and he is a good boss. It was comforting knowing I had a job to return to whether I failed or completed my thru-hike. Either way, it was good to know I would be able to pay off my REI bill someday.

I guess I could have done some training to get ready for this hike but as I mentioned it was the winter from hell. The snow had been

Pre-hike gear check in Connecticut

piling up for months and with all the shoveling, carrying firewood and windshield scraping I had been doing, I felt pretty good. When you spend a whole weekend shoveling snow off your Dad's barn to prevent it from collapsing, you get quite a workout. Hiking was out of the question. The woods had a minimum of four feet of snow and the mailman was using a grabber-stick to deliver the mail because the roads were getting so narrow from the giant snowbanks. Hiking on the roads was just too dangerous. Going to the gym and using an elliptical machine would have been good, too, but it was so cold just walking out to the truck would throw my lungs into an asthma attack. I couldn't wait to get to Georgia.

The day I left for the airport it was snowy and gray and there was a threat of flight cancellations. I wasn't on a tight schedule but I wanted to get started without any delays. Besides, I was pretty sick of the snow and was looking forward to getting somewhere warm. I stuffed my new backpack and all my gear into a camouflage hunting duffel, and checked it in at the gate. It weighed forty-one pounds. With all my new hiking clothes on, I hiked my way to the security checkpoint where I spent the next hour being frisked, x-rayed, metal-detected and questioned. Eventually I got on the plane. We sat there parked for what seemed like hours. I stared out the little window watching the snow pile up outside. At one point I thought the plane was on fire because a crew of Eskimo firefighters started spraying the plane! Thankfully, they were just de-icing it because we got clearance from the tower for take-off. When the tires lifted off the ground, I felt like my adventure had finally begun.

1

Adventure Begins

 In case you don't already know, the AT doesn't begin at the Atlanta airport. No. It is about 100 miles away in Fannin County. The first thing I did was retrieve my hiking gear from the carousel, remove my backpack from the duffel bag and throw the duffel in a garbage can. This drew the attention of a security guard and after some explaining and a thorough inspection of the discarded duffel as well as my new backpack, I was allowed to leave. They must not have been hikers like me because while I was describing what a "Leave No Trace" trowel was, they just told me to get going. "Take a hike," I think he said. Everyone is a comedian.

I was given some pretty specific instructions by a shuttle service where to go to be picked up. I had to take the public transportation, a train, to the end of the line and wait for them there. My pick up wasn't for a few hours so I decided to find a Walmart and stock up on food for the first leg of my hike. Luckily there was one slightly out of the way, so I got off the train a few stops early and started my first official hike. I had to hike about a mile. Normally I would consider this a walk on a sidewalk, but with my new backpack, boots and $130 trekking poles, there was no denying that I was hiking. I got quite a few looks. I guess there aren't a lot of hikers in Atlanta. I was so happy to be hiking on bare concrete I could barely compose my smile. By the time I reached Walmart, my Smartwool was starting to heat up; it was in the mid-thirties and I wasn't used to this kind of heat! When I got to the doors of Walmart I faced my first hurdle. There, taped to the door, was a sign: NO BACKPACKS IN STORE. I guess there are a lot of hikers in Atlanta after all. The manager at the desk told me it would be all right, so I placed it in my cart and went in.

I was getting pretty hungry by then and I thought, "If I'm this hungry from flying, I'll be even more hungry from hiking." So I stocked up with extra food.

My hike back to the train was somewhat encumbered by the two big blue bags I was carrying my food in, and I looked forward to getting to the hostel where I was planning to stay for the night. I was going to be shuttled to Springer Mountain in the morning, so I would have plenty of time to put my food in my new food bag this evening. Being from rural Connecticut, I wasn't used to the city and I have to admit, I was a little clumsy trying to sit on the train with a big backpack, two poles and two bags of food. I already missed my truck. I eventually made it to my pick-up spot and the shuttle driver arrived right on time. The first thing she asked me was if I needed to get anything at Walmart. I guess she didn't notice the two big blue bags with smiley faces on them. I thanked her, smiled and said no, then popped open one of my Dr. Peppers and sat back to enjoy the ride.

This was my first experience staying in a hostel. A hostel is an economical alternative to a motel. They are cheaper, usually have amenities geared toward hikers like laundry, Wi-Fi, meals and showers.

The lodging, however, usually involves many people sleeping in bunk rooms. This hostel was very nice. It was clean, the people were very nice and welcoming, and I shared the basement with a nice lady from France. The other hikers that were there were all excited to start their own thru-hike attempt. I was no longer a K-9 officer or an auto tech. I was a hiker and I was with my own kind. While they all sat around talking about some trail called the El Capitan Sauvignon Blanc or something in Spain, I was getting all my food in my pack and trying to zip, pull cords and clip it up.

When they noticed me grunting and pulling my pack together, the topic of discussion turned to pack weight. I was surprised to hear that all these people had packs that seemed light to me. Surely they hadn't met the specialists at REI or maybe they didn't have an REI wherever they were from. I became worried for their well-being. They convinced me to weigh my pack and they were aghast when they saw it was 52 pounds After they all calmed down and showered me with their hiking credentials, I conceded to shave a few pounds off and send some stuff home. The hostel owners said they would be sure to get my things in the mail and gave me a box. So I began.

I decided to start with the non-essentials: cribbage board, salt and pepper shaker, coffee creamer, ace bandages, three pairs of socks, and two bottles of Dr. Pepper. I was told that I wouldn't need that much food, but I just bought it so I wasn't ready to take it out. I repacked my backpack and I had shaved off three pounds. With some frustration I would repeat this three more times before I was sure I needed everything in my pack. Final weight: 47 pounds. Time to get some sleep; it was going to be a big day tomorrow.

All my fellow hikers were up early and we had a big breakfast of pancakes and eggs as part of our shuttle/hostel deal, and we were packed into a van and headed off to Springer Mountain. You could feel the anticipation. It took about an hour of bouncing around on dirt roads, but we eventually arrived at the trailhead where I got to see my first white blaze.

We all got out of the van and unloaded our packs. With well-wishing and handshakes, we drifted apart to check our gear, adjust straps, read the trailhead kiosk and head out. I read all the notices about "Leave No Trace," "Bear Awareness" and shuttle services. When I looked at the map on the information board I learned that I hadn't actually been dropped off at the beginning of the AT. The beginning of the AT was at the top of Springer Mountain and I had to hike south for about a mile before I could start! I was anxious to start this hike and I didn't mind the warm up hike in Atlanta, but it seemed like I would never get turned north and begin!

Reluctantly, I turned south and headed up to the summit of Springer to get started. All the way up, every step, all I could think of was, "These steps don't count, these steps don't count." I guess it is common to have family to join you on Springer, because each time I stopped on the trail to catch my breath, people dressed in jeans and sneakers passed me. A few would stop to see if I was okay. While talking with them, they would tell me they were only hiking this stretch to snap a picture of their family member and see them off. I think they were just using me as an excuse to stop hiking for a moment and admire my state-of-the-art hiking gear.

I finally arrived at the beginning of the Appalachian Trail. I stood on the rock summit of Springer Mountain, the southern terminus of the longest hiking-only trail in the world. I was almost overcome with emotion; after all, I had been planning this moment for weeks. My legs were shaking a little, partly from my excitement, partly from the mile hike. I set my pack down to take in the moment, savor the view and catch my breath. I hung my Smartwool "outer layer" on a branch to dry and opened a Dr. Pepper to celebrate.

People who have been to Connecticut, especially the rural farmlands in the northeast corner of the state, will tell you how beautiful it is. Standing on top of Springer, I wasn't impressed. I snapped a picture with my phone, waited in line to sign the hiker logbook and decided it was time to start north. There was a small crowd there and I felt a twinge of sadness watching the families as they said goodbye to their hikers. Sons, daughters, even some kids seeing off their father. They were all taking pictures, hugging and wiping tears. I realized at that moment that this was the first adventure I was doing without my boys since they were born. Not to get to sappy, but I missed my dog then, too.

Hoisting my pack on, I started the first few steps north in a mellow mood accompanied by the rhythmic crinkling of an empty Dr. Pepper bottle coming from my pack.

There was a lot of excitement on the trail. The first mile seemed very familiar and I passed many people heading to the top of Springer. I felt like a trail expert having already been there. When people passed me going up, I answered a common question that I would hear hundreds of times before reaching Maine, "How far?" In my most enthusiastic voice I'd say, "Almost there." It meant "about a mile." Soon enough I was back at the trailhead where it had turned into chaos. There were vans of hikers being dropped off, cars of supportive, teary-eyed family members trying to turn around to head back down the dirt road, and cars full of soon-to-be, teary-eyed family members trying to cram into the small lot. I was glad to be heading north, to Maine.

I must be honest here – I was very excited myself. My mood had lifted since I left the summit and I was feeling better now that the miles were starting to add up. I knew at this rate I'd be a thru-hiker soon. It was getting near lunchtime and I decided to stop for a break. The weather became unusually warm, in the high sixties. Even the people from the south were talking about how warm it was. According to the experts on the trail, it had been a rainy winter and that was why the trails were so muddy and slick. There were many experts. I didn't want to be a know-it-all, but I had seen the videos on YouTube, been taught by the experts at REI and did a fair bit of hiking in Atlanta before I even arrived "on-trail." I even thought I was a bit more qualified than most of the other hikers because I was almost 50 years old and had been walking twice as long as most of the hikers were alive.

I picked a nice little spot for a break that was very inviting. It was quite open, just a few steps off the trail. There were a few large logs forming a perfect natural campsite and someone had built a stone campfire pit in the middle. The area was free of brush and twigs. In fact, there wasn't a dead stick within 50 yards of the camp. The area had been picked clean of anything that would qualify as campfire material. A few other hikers joined me and before long there were several more sharing this spot. This is when I got my first real taste of true hiker trail-talk.

I sat listening like they were speaking a different language. They were throwing terms around and talking strategies, mileage schedules and completion dates! That's when I realized my strategy was different than most. My strategy, if I had one, was to have minimal strategy. I wasn't being careless or reckless. I had a trail guide so I could plan resupply stops and properly load up for the next section. I planned to use it when I needed to find water. I also wanted to track my progress. Other than that guide for reference, I planned to hike until I was tired, hang my hammock and camp. Naturally, I would pay attention to nutrition, hydration, weather, hazards, etc., but I was in no rush. As far as planning a finish date, that seemed extreme.

I was enjoying this gathering immensely because I could see the excitement and enthusiasm in everyone sitting around. The icebreaker among fellow hikers who are not yet acquainted, starts with three core questions: What is your trail name? Where are you from? What is your pack weight? It's fascinating when you think about it. Total strangers are able to jump into a quite comfortable conversation based on those three questions, and one known common interest. As a hiker, no one teaches you these questions. I didn't hear it mentioned in any of my research, but when you find yourself out there with so many people, doing the same thing and with the same ultimate goal in mind, you want to know. Brief conversations between passing hikers as well as lifelong friendships have been started with these three questions.

"What is your trail name?"

This is usually the first question asked when meeting another hiker. It is the ultimate icebreaker because eventually everyone gets one and they are interesting, often clever, and in most cases, unique to the bearer of the name. No one knows why this trail tradition began, but according to Larry Luxenberg from the Appalachian Trail Museum, Earl Shaffer, the first person to walk the entire trail, called himself "The Crazy One." That was in 1948, and although not everyone had a trail name as recent as the eighties, they are standard practice now.

A trail name, in its rawest definition is a hiker's new identity. They have left their jobs, homes, schools, families and friends, and have begun a temporary new life as a hiker. For the next foreseeable future, the title you wore and the name you were given at birth can be set aside. It's a fun tradition and I'm sure a shrink would have a field day trying to explain it. Generally, a trail name is given to a hiker by other hikers. Some hikers name themselves rather than get stuck with a less desirable name. A few get their trail name within hours of getting to the trail, others can go weeks. A single act or a behavior can be trail name worthy. "Tunez," got his name because he listened to music while he hiked. "Walnut," because his wife sent him walnuts. "Ukalady" carried a ukulele. "Piper," "Fiddler" and "Stache" each carried their namesake. "Easy Go" was easy going, and everyone with the name "Turtle" or "Caboose" were generally slow. "Tortis," despite his trail name, was a very fast hiker. "Easy Strider" got his trail name from "Animal."

Geography plays a large role when trail names are concerned. Home pride is strong. "Yukon," "Oriole," "Chicago," "Chesapeake" and "Tucson" were proud to carry their homes' name, but some took it a step further like "Sota-Sam," "Miami Vice," "Boston Mule" and "Big Easy." Trail names like these eliminated the second icebreaker question, "Where are you from?" and skipped right to the pack weight question. More on that in a few minutes.

There were some familiar trail names as well: "BlueRiver-Phoenix," "Kris Kristofferson," "Willie Nelson" and "Waylon Jennings." There was even a German postman named "Hasselhoff."

You are probably getting the idea. When you get your trail name by other hikers, interestingly, you are named by how they see you. The opposite is true when you name yourself. Perhaps it is how you want to be seen: "Free Bird," "Funemployed," "Dusty Pilgrim" (from Plymouth, Massachusetts), "BeerMan" and "Warm and Toasty," to name a few. "Bean Counter" was an accountant.

One hiker, "Bismark," used his trail name for anonymity. I jokingly called him "Brunswick" because the second time we met I accidentally called him that, and it remained a running joke between us. The last time I saw him in person was just outside Damascus, Virginia. He was camped with a couple I had been leap-frogging all day, and they all planned to go into town the following morning. The next time I saw him was on the news. While in Damascus he was arrested for stealing over $8 million from one of the big soda companies. His trail name and hiker lifestyle had kept him out of the hands of the law for several years.

Whatever your trail name and however you get it, it is a fun part of the trail culture. It's like two people who pass on the road riding Harley Davidsons. One may be a teacher and the other a truck driver. They wave to each other because, for that instant in time, they share a common interest. It is the same on the trail.

My trail name is "Sam I Am."

All mentioned trail names were actual hikers last year. Some I don't even know their real names. You will get to know a few of them as you read on. A few of them will remain my lifelong friends.

"Where are you from?"

Hiking the AT brings on thoughts of solitude, serenity and relaxation. While I was planning, those thoughts were my motivating factors. After all, they are the reasons Benton MacKaye envisioned the trail in the first place; "an escape from the evils of modern life." Much has changed since 1921. The first thing I noticed was the sheer numbers of hikers on the trail. Starting in Georgia in mid-March makes sense for a number of reasons: it is spring, the weather is mild and the timing puts you in Maine before winter hits. Many people opt for alternative hikes, doing specific sections in a well-planned order, or they start in the north and finish in the south. Most, however, start in Georgia. This makes the trail very crowded. When I found myself sharing a footpath with that many people, I became curious where they all came from. This curiosity was common among hikers, which is the reason for Icebreaker #2: "Where are you from?"

Referring to last year's Appalachian Trail Conservancy's (ATC) list of 2000 Milers, most states are represented. Naturally, the states that are most commonly represented are those that we call "Trail States," those that we hike through. These hikers often have a connection to the trail having hiked and camped on it with scouts, family or friends. International hikers are also drawn to the trail because of its rugged appeal and reputation for its beauty and wildness. I found that Germans are the most common of the international hikers, but occasionally you would meet someone from Australia, UK or Canada. For international hikers though, time is more critical. They often get a six-month visa and have to complete their hike before their deadline. That doesn't leave much time to nurse an injury or go sightseeing off the trail. Fortunately for them, Washington, D.C., and New York City are close to the trail if they want to stop. "Happy," from New Zealand, still wearing his hiking clothes, was on a plane from Boston heading home within hours of finishing his thru-hike.

The popularity of long distance hiking has grown recently. The release of books and movies, along with the explosion of outdoor sports enthusiasts wanting to get back to nature, has turned the AT into a very busy and crowded place. It is especially busy in Georgia during spring. Icebreaker #2 also helps remember the answer to Icebreaker #1. For example: "Still Phil" from Germany or "Jeopardy" from Baltimore. Fun, isn't it?

"What is your pack weight?"

The trail teaches you not to judge. It is the great equalizer. Age, gender, nationality, professions and cultural differences no longer define who we are. Eventually you learn not to judge. It is a unique environment when that happens. Each of us had to grasp the iron bars to climb near Dragon's Tooth, and we all walked on the same bridges to cross New Jersey's swamps. When we navigated the Mahoosuc Notch, we all slowed to a crawl. The rain soaked us all and we each lost sleep because a whippoorwill decided to announce his presence during the night. After a few weeks, we even begin to look and smell like each other! There are thousands of steps and handholds that each and every hiker used. I guess what I am trying to illustrate is that we are all in the same boat. No matter why we're here, how we got here or where we go when we're through, we are equal on the trail. That lesson doesn't actually happen right away. It takes a few weeks to realize that there is no chain of command, no social classes and no judgment. We all pull our packs on the same way and we all poop in the woods.

In the beginning, however, there is a whole lot of judging going on. Maybe it is nerves, maybe it is excitement or maybe hikers just like to talk about pack weight. Whatever the reason, hikers sure want to know. I don't think they actually cared about the actual weight – it was an icebreaker. This question leads directly into the second most talked about subject on the AT... Gear.

You are a hiker now. You live in the woods, hike up mountains and down mountains, just like everyone else in your new world. One thing, other than your trail name, that makes you unique is your gear. There is so much gear on the market it would boggle your mind. Hikers love their gear! A gear conversation also lets the experts impress you with their vast knowledge of hiking. I sleep in a hammock. I'm comfortable in a hammock. That was my whole thought process, so I

Springer Mountain

brought my hammock. I even brought cotton long johns to sleep in. I like long johns. The experts don't like long johns. They do like to give advice though. I got advice on fabric, food, what pack I should have gotten, my footwear, the estimated mileage I should shoot for, what towns to go to, the weather and so on.

I enjoy meeting new people and sharing conversation, but the gear talk was nonstop and I found it to be equal to measuring penises. I carried what I wanted and it weighed what it weighed. If anyone asks you how much your pack weighs, be prepared to be judged. You

SAM "SAM I AM" DUCHARME

won't be asked that after the first couple weeks – no one cares after that. They will want to know how many miles you are doing today and where you camped. More measuring...

2

Back to the Trail

Fascinating as it was to interact with the other hikers, I had to get back to hiking. The next few days would be eye-opening for me. The trail was wet and slippery but not particularly difficult. I leapfrogged the same dozen hikers throughout the first day exchanging pleasantries and encouragement. When I stopped for a breather, they would pass me and I'd find myself passing them when they stopped to rest. The trail was two feet wide, compacted soil and wound its way along the mountain. Gradually, it gained elevation until it crested and descended the mountain on the other side. I felt great to be walking through the forest surrounded by gigantic hardwoods. The trees hadn't begun to bud yet and the forest floor was still a carpet of brown leaves except for the dark path I was walking on.

The sun shined through the bare branches and the trail made a long scar through the woods. I could see a scattering of colorful dots which were hikers with their bright packs and hiking clothes. Happy to be away from New England and the snow, I was in heaven. After learning that I had only hiked three miles before lunch break, I concentrated on hiking out the rest of the day. It was a late start and hiking south to begin my trip guaranteed me a short first day. The climbs continued to be gradual and occasionally I would hike through an area with rhododendrons which gave the forest some color. The different tones of green leaves hung limply on the cold branches waiting for spring to arrive. I hiked throughout the rest of the day happy to be alive and anxious to reach the first campsite of my hike.

The "experts" kept me briefed on my progress during the day. I was informed of a shelter ahead which had a water source. Hikers don't call them streams; they are water sources, something I'd have to remember. When I arrived at the shelter, I was amazed at the number of people who were setting up camp! There were tents and people everywhere! I noticed several hammocks strung up between trees and the shelter itself was packed with hikers. I'm a social guy but I had a plan for camping. "Loner," my all-time favorite YouTube personality, taught me about "stealth-camping." He thru-hiked in 2012 and basically, it means camping wherever you want. I called it "camping wherever you want." This fit my style because I knew I was out of shape and would need my rest. Sleeping away from people would ensure I wouldn't be disturbed. I also wanted to be able to bathe every night, and being by myself afforded me the ability to take a baby-wipe bath without offending other hikers with my nudity. Laugh now, but I'm serious about my hygiene!

I decided to hike down to the "water-source" and fill up on water. I planned to return to the trail then continue north until I found a nice place to camp. The stream was a little off-trail and I decided to bring my pack with me. This turned out to be a good idea because I found a great spot to camp in the woods near the stream. I filtered some water with my new filtration system and settled in for some supper.

Stealth camping

It was still early so I hung my hammock in some rhododendrons to claim a spot and found a nice place to cook. I should have practiced using my stove before I headed into the wilderness. I made a stove out of beer cans like I saw on YouTube, and a windscreen made from tin foil. Both of which are important if you want to eat hot food on the trail. It took me several times to get my stove lit and when I finally got it burning correctly, I ran out of fuel before the water came to a boil! I tried again and finally was able to eat a meal of rice and sausage. I wasn't that hungry with all the excitement of the day but I ate anyway burning my mouth in the process.

I met many more hikers who came down for water. The first comment they made was how smart I was to camp down here away from the crowd. I led on about how I always do this, like I knew it all along. My site was only 1/10th from the trail, or "point-1" in hiker talk, and I was completely alone. Just up the trail near the shelter, however, there were 50 hikers camped. I knew then that I would "stealth camp" every night. I was tired from hiking and climbed into my hammock.

It was March and the days were still relatively short so I welcomed the chance to go to sleep early. Before I turned off my headlight, however, I decided to take a look at my trail guide to estimate my day's mileage. It had been a long day, the hills were continuous and I felt like I had accomplished a hard day's work. Maybe I would take it easy tomorrow, I heard some hikers overdo it in the beginning, knocking out big days and ending up getting injuries. I didn't want that. I already decided that regardless how many miles I did today; I was going to cut it down to ten tomorrow. Close examination of my trail guide showed that my first day hiking the AT amounted to seven miles! 2182.2 miles to go! I was crushed.

I slept well the first night. I always sleep well in my hammock. I sleep even better when it is near a babbling stream. I heard some hikers chatting about hiking gear as they got water, and I decided to get up. Packing my camp took a while, and then I got some water and headed back to the trail. When I got there it looked like the day after the circus. All the tents were gone, there were no hikers around, and the place was deserted! My watch showed 8 a.m., and I was the last to leave.

Day 2 started out a little slow. My calves hurt and I was having a slow time adjusting to a trail condition called a "Gap." As you know, the Appalachian Trail runs the length of the Appalachian Mountain Range. In the course of hiking the trail you are tasked with the pleasure of crossing 300 peaks. The peaks in the beginning are lower than those in the north, and they are soil covered, allowing trees to grow at the very top, affording you few views. It's what's between the mountains that I was struggling with. The lowest point between two mountains is called a "gap." The gaps were killing me! Although the mountains aren't as high as those in the north, they are steep! Each gap had a name and some had a road splitting the mountains, but there was no rest. You hiked straight up out of a gap, over a top and straight back down!

My legs were turning into jello with each step. By mid-morning I was hiking among other hikers and when I looked up the hillsides leading out of a gap, I could see the trail lined with gasping hikers sitting on rock steps and others standing, leaning forward on their poles trying to catch their breath. I knew both positions well; I had been alternating between them. I couldn't believe how physically demanding this was! I knew I hadn't had time to train and I knew I was out of shape, but Holy Crap! My lungs were on fire! My legs were very shaky. By lunchtime I was starting to buckle on some of the downhill steps. It was time to stop and fuel up.

My enthusiasm for the three icebreakers was temporarily on hold as I stuffed a couple of Cliff Bars in my mouth and made a tuna and Slim Jim tortilla. I don't know if yesterday's adrenalin wore off or if it was possible that I was this out of shape, but I was going through a state of panic knowing this was only 11:00 a.m. on Day 2! I was seriously wondering if I was going to be on the wrong side of the 75%/25% ratio of thru-hike completion statistics. I stood up, determined to continue, when I decided a few extra minutes of rest probably wouldn't affect my summit date on Katahdin. I sat back down.

According to the ATC almost 50% of thru-hikes end before the halfway point and a high number of those end in the first 40 miles.

I was beginning to realize why. I was in disbelief as to how strenuous hiking was! I was also questioning myself whether I had made a mistake. Camping, living with limited comforts and dealing with the elements were all things I embraced. This hiking, however, proved to be harder than it looked! I found myself embarrassed on several occasions when I was pathetically winded, and leaned forward on my poles desperately sucking air.

I continued on, wondering how the trail, so friendly and mild with its long meandering curves and easy slopes, could turn so ugly. Sharp rock steps built into endless stairs threatened to tear at me with the slightest fall. The steep descents were pounding my legs with each footfall. Instead of hearing birds chirping, all I could hear was my loud huffing and puffing! There were times I could hear my own heart beating inside my ears. It was pure torture!

Thankfully, the trail followed the ridgetop and returned to its gentler ways, and I was able to keep going. I decided to re-explore my hiking goals. Did I really have to go all the way to Maine? Who was I trying to impress? Who would I disappoint? I decided to go on. My goal, however, changed. I decided to take it one day at a time, one hill at a time. When I had enough, I'd go home. For now, I'd hike until nightfall.

My pace slowed and I was less miserable on the flat ridgetops. The gaps were less frequent and the spacing between them gave me some time to recover. I was still moving forward, albeit, slowly. Eventually I arrived at a shelter. Having enough hiking for one day and seeing the area filled with hikers, I decided to pass the shelter and start looking for a good place to stealth camp. Despite my weary legs, I decided to climb up a mountain to watch the sun come up in the morning. I left the trail and hiked about "point-3" to the top of a nearby mountain where I set up my hammock, hung my sweat soaked clothes, gave myself a baby wipe bath and went to sleep without supper. I know now that not eating is a rookie hiking mistake, but what did you expect from a rookie hiker?

Winter temperatures had returned during the night and I woke to a cold world. It was already 8 a.m. and I missed the sunrise. When I stepped out of my hammock wearing my cotton long johns, I walked through the crunchy leaves and pulled my frozen hiking clothes off the branches of a nearby tree. Besides rendering my toes frozen, my little foray out of bed made me acutely aware of my sore legs. I was disappointed to miss the sunrise. I had slept later than I hoped, my legs hurt and I was hungry. I changed into my frozen hiking clothes, pulled on my lightweight hiking jacket and packed up. As I munched on an energy bar, I hoisted my pack for my third day on the trail and headed down the mountain.

At the risk of losing readers who might call BS here, I assure you the following is NOT a dramatization: I got lost! At first I didn't think I was lost. No lost person does. Not until I had hiked a full fifteen minutes did I start thinking, "I should see the trail by now." I gave it a few more minutes but I still hadn't reached the trail. No problem. I was just distracted in thought and veered off course. I retraced my steps planning to start over when I saw something familiar. My problem began when I didn't see anything familiar. The first lesson when you get lost is "don't panic." I don't panic often and I was fine at the moment, but I couldn't shake the feeling that if my hunting buddies ever found out about this, my reputation was over. I didn't have any clue what I was doing. My newly formulated plan was to walk all the way back up, find my campsite and start over. I practice "Leave No Trace." It means take out what you take in, don't chop trees down and don't start forest fires. I'm very good at Leave No Trace. In fact, I'm so good at it I couldn't even find my campsite.

I couldn't be that lost. I camped less than a half mile from at least 50 hikers! I listened, but being deaf in one ear was a disadvantage. I couldn't hear anyone. I circled the top of the mountain. No help. Here I was, a former K-9 officer, a certified finder of people, lost. How embarrassing.

I decided to use the top of the mountain and walk straight down for 20 minutes. If I don't cross the trail, I'll climb back up and repeat in a different direction. This time I left a trace. I scuffed my feet disturbing the leaves so I could ensure I walked straight, I would look back and adjust my course as needed. I could also follow my back tracks to where I started. In a worst case scenario, if I had a heart attack and died, I'd be easy to find from the air. I chuckled thinking about the conclusion the detectives would arrive at: Suicide by mountain.

I was getting tired and I was losing my humor, but I kept at it for about 45 minutes and eventually I came out on the trail just as a young lady with purple hair was hiking by. I took one look at her and said, "Boy, am I happy to see you!" She smiled and replied, "I'm happy to see you, too!" She nervously stepped around this overly happy, grinning man who jumped out of the bushes in front of her, and continued down the trail. I was again happy to be alive and didn't give a thought to how creepy that must have been for her. (Incidentally, if you talk to any of my hunting buddies please don't repeat this story.)

Night

As you can see, my first few days on the trail were harsh lessons on what I had gotten myself into. But I'm a stubborn man and I continued to hike on, paying for all my sins and shortcomings in life with burning lungs and agonizing legs. My determination to get through the day was only slightly stronger than my determination to quit. Both determinations were almost equal.

I won't drag you through each day; this book would be ridiculously repetitive and boring. However, the third night is worth mentioning. "Night," in a backpacker's world, starts when you decide to stop hiking for the day. "Hiker midnight" is a term that describes the time when all hikers are in their sleeping bag for the night. More often than not, hiker midnight occurs at sunset. Sunset is called "sunset."

At the end of Day 3 I found myself near a water source. There wasn't a shelter but according to "Carusoe," there was a campsite. The site was a bit off the trail so I decided to look for a place to camp. Carusoe was from West Virginia and he liked to talk about gear. It was hard to follow his conversation with his hard southern accent, but once he removed his bug net I was able to read his lips. He was a hammocker and it was the one piece of gear I was familiar enough with that I could pull my own weight in a conversation. I thought it would be nice to camp with him and his son "Colt 45," so we got our water and continued to the campsite. According to the app on his smartphone, this site could accommodate quite a few hikers, but on arriving there, it was no more than a flat strip of ground resembling an old logging road. On that road we found over a hundred campers already set up. After a full day of hiking through dull gray forests and brown leaf hills, the color explosion of tents looked absurd in the woods.

An advantage to hammocking is that you can camp almost anywhere. Luckily, Colt 45 found a place to squeeze his tent between two other campers, but Carusoe and I were forced to seek a spot on a steep hillside above camp to hang our hammocks. The forest floor was blanketed with soft oak leaves and trees were plentiful, so finding a good spot was easy. Being away from the other hikers appealed to me for all the reasons I mentioned before. However, setting up my camp on a hillside with the roof pitch of a colonial-style house has its drawbacks. To begin with, my legs were tired – very tired. I was finding it difficult to stand on such a steep angle. Each time I dropped something it rolled all the way to the campers below. After two or three trips I decided to wait until I was finished hanging my hammock and then retrieve my sleeping bag, clothes bag, food bag and titanium cup. (The new bags I bought at REI certainly had a way of rolling down hills.) Happy with my "hang," I climbed into my hammock and watched as Carusoe attempted to defy physics and finish with his hammock.

I'm a believer that in life, many experiences, whether good or bad, can be attributed to being in the right place at the right time. On my third night on the trail, lying in my hammock on that hillside, less than an hour after meeting Carusoe and Colt 45, I was in the right place.

Don't let anyone tell you that hanging a food bag is easy. Of course everything gets easier with practice, but to the unpracticed, hanging a food bag can be difficult. I can't stress the importance of hanging your food from a tree when in the forest. There are animals in the woods who would love to have a night off from scavenging or hunting and for them, getting into your food bag is even better than finding a rotten beaver carcass on a stump. After eating a few easy meals of sweet power bars and Jack Links Beef Jerky, grubs lose their flair.

It was this attention to responsible backcountry camping that my new trail friend Carusoe entertained me with for the next 45 minutes. As per hiking fashion, following his hammock hang, Carusoe set out to hang his food bag. A careful evaluation of suitable branches was conducted and a limb was selected. The limb seemed strong enough and the rope sailed over the branch with ease. However, when the rope was pulled to raise the bulging bag, the inadequate branch strained

and bent, ultimately touching the ground. I was eating my second peanut butter and pepperoni tortilla, and offered tips from my hammock.

The second limb was a brute. At 20 feet up it would protect that
food from any woodland creature short of Bigfoot himself. Getting
a rope over the limb requires a weight tied to the end of the rope, a
good arm, coordination and a little luck. Carusoe had a small rock for
weight, period. He lacked the coordination and luck. His first throw
was a piece of beauty and the rock with the rope sailed through the air
perfectly cresting over the limb. Just as it was completing its ark, the
rope went taught and the rock looped several time around the limb
wrapping the rope like the stripes on a barbershop pole. Those people
who have found themselves in this unenviable position know that it
renders the rope static, strike two. When Carusoe glanced over to see
if I saw it, I looked away.

After soliciting the help from his son Colt 45, they attempted
to free the rope with long sticks. It took some engineering and some
imagination, but they finally succeeded and prepared for another
attempt. The next throw was short lived because with all the looking
up, neither noticed the bright orange rope was wrapped around Colt
45's foot. That rock went about four feet before it shot back at them
causing both to dive for cover. Strike three. This was the most fun I
had all day!

At this point Carusoe was getting pretty stressed out and started
taking his frustration out on his son. He had been standing on that
side hill for a while now and it was putting quite a strain on his legs.
Colt 45 took matters into his own hands by taking a turn at throwing. His throw was absolutely perfect. The rock was expertly thrown
and uninhibited by anything... including the rope, which came off. I
couldn't contain myself any longer and burst out laughing. I felt the
tension from their glares and for a moment, it was like a Mexican

standoff. I couldn't help finding the whole situation, spiraling out of control, absolutely hysterical, and as hard as I tried, I couldn't stop. Luckily, laughter is contagious and it cracked the tension. Soon we were all laughing. My legs were so sore I couldn't offer to help so I continued to bark out advice from my hammock.

A few minutes before it was completely dark they managed to get that skinny little rope over the branch. When I asked them if they minded clipping my food bag to theirs, the laughter began all over. Being nice guys, they agreed. They even got my bag from me so I didn't have to get out of my comfy hammock. The last thing I remember seeing before drifting off to sleep was a line of tents lit up in the darkness. From above, they looked like big colorful lamps trailing into the forest.

I guess I should have taken a trip to the little boy's tree before I went to sleep because around 3 a.m. I had to pee. Peeing in the woods is easy. Basically, you stop and pee. Some discretion is used in the presence of others; other than that, nature does most of the work. You would think peeing under the cover of darkness would be even easier, but that didn't prove to be the case in the wee hours of my third night in the woods.

Throughout the last three days I had over worked my pale weak legs. The climbs slowly became unbearable, and even the smallest hills took several rest stops to conquer. I was struggling with the downhills as well, experiencing weakness, and occasionally they would just buckle like I was genuflecting in a Catholic church. I attributed it to the heavy pack. Needless to say, my muscles were very sore, especially my calves. We've all been there, suffering for a few days when we start going to the gym again. (Generally this occurs on January 2, 3 and 4.) If you have never worked out, it goes like this: First day after stiff; second day after sore; third day after incapacitated. I'm no muscleoligist, but that is the way muscles work.

I had a pair of crocs on the ground by my hammock; "camp shoes" the experts called them. I sat sideways on my hammock, and in one motion, I slid my toes into the crocs and stood. Within a nanosecond my world was turned upside down. Excruciating pain shot through my calves. I couldn't straighten my legs! My brain, in an attempt to preserve itself, jolted my body back as if I had stepped on an electric eel! Between the steep hillside, my physically impaired legs, and my wimpy beam of light, I was going down fast! I should have just dove for my hammock. Instead, I sealed my own fate; I attempted to save myself. Losing my balance, my right foot shot out and flung my croc into the darkness. I was clawing at my tarp trying to claim my footing when I realized all hope was lost. I could hear a few of my things bounding down the hill towards the campers below as I stumbled through the crunchy leaves and sticks, eventually succumbing to gravity. I was pretty scratched up but unhurt and glad that it was over. It must have sounded like two bull elk fighting up on that hill, with all the crashing and thrashing. I'm sure those elk let out a swear or two also. I wouldn't know – my legs hurt so bad I think I blacked out.

I didn't even try to stand up to pee. I just remained on my knees and held onto a nearby oak. I then followed the trail of disturbed ground back to my hammock and lay down. I nearly cried from the relief when I got off my feet. I could hear Carusoe laughing from his hammock. I was trying to figure a way to blame the disturbance on him when people asked in the morning. I never got that chance. He already told them by the time I got up.

It didn't take me long to learn that if you sleep close to the crowd, you are not sleeping late. I'm not a late sleeper. I'm talking six-thirty or seven. In the backpacker world that is late. When your daily pro-duction is measured in miles it's good to get an early start. I wasn't going anywhere soon because throughout the night my legs continued to become more uncomfortable. That is the nice way of saying they hurt like hell! I was experiencing pain, swelling, muscle spasms and an inability to move the muscles in my legs. Basically, I was stuck in my hammock! I remembered an acronym I learned from the internet to assist in my treatment: "RICE" Rest. Ice. Compression. Elevation. I'm sure it was the Elevation that caused all the trouble! I regretted sending my ace bandages home. As for rest, I wasn't leaving until the mouthful of ibuprofen kicked in any way. (Hiking is so fun.)

I was also learning why the first campsite looked so deserted after the first night on the trail. From my position high enough to see at least half of the tents, I watched the camp come to life. The first few people woke in the pre-dawn, shining their head lamps like search lights. This activity stirred the camp and soon there were people walk-ing around, cooking breakfast and packing their tents. I could tell they were trying to be quiet but in the still of the morning, whispers carry as far as outright talking. From what I could tell from my perch in the trees, they were talking about their gear. As the sun rose and the camp became light, most campers were up, preparing for the day's hike. I had the occasional visitor when a hiker would climb the hill to return one of my belongings that rolled into their tent during the night. Most just wanted to know what all the commotion was around 3 a.m.

Within an hour after light, the camp was empty except for Colt 45's tent, Carusoe and I. It seemed that Carusoe was dealing with some leg pain of his own and was in no rush to set out. Colt 45 was used to sleeping late and hadn't heard a thing all morning. Our hammocks were close enough to talk back and forth, and we covered the three icebreakers, leading to other topics, and forging the beginning of a close friendship.

We talked until mid-morning and decided to pack up and head out. I let my backpack roll to the bottom of the hill, grabbed my hammock and sleeping bag in my arms, and slid to the bottom on my butt looking for my other croc on the way down. We woke Colt 45 and slowly limped out of camp.

Moose poop

3

Poop in the Woods

Following my thru-hike, I began taking the trail to the people. I conducted numerous programs, used social media, podcasts and radio interviews. Inevitably, one reoccurring topic would come up: pooping in the woods. For us Americans, it seems primitive; after all, we live in the 21st century. I don't know why this is such an awkward topic. I can think of several other places where it is more uncomfortable to go. Remember when you first started dating and would leave the house halfway through the movie rather than use the bathroom at your sweetheart's house? How about at the game where there are hundreds of fans lined up and there are no doors on the stalls? And who wants to use the guest bathroom at a party when everyone in attendance will know how long you take, how bad you smell and how many times you flush? Yes, there are way more uncomfortable places to poop than the woods.

Just like everything else relating to long-distance backpacking, you have to have a plan. The plan you go with should be based on thorough research, product testing and field testing. On one occasion, I left my pack on the trail because I was in such a hurry and I forgot my post-poop supplies. I had to rely on my back up plan. (Somewhere in Pennsylvania there is a Darn Tough, low-cut sock decomposing in a hole.)

There are techniques that you should be familiar with and those techniques should be practiced. It is important to recognize which technique is called for in any given situation and that a certain skill level be attained before attempting it out in the backcountry. It should be noted that whatever technique you choose, there are certain risks involved. For instance, the unpracticed person may poop on his or her own foot. You would never do that, right? Wait until one of the pricker bushes you tramped down on the way in, suddenly springs back to life while you are least expecting it! If the sudden thorn to the backside doesn't make you jump, a bee or snake will!

If the wrong technique is attempted for the terrain, it could result in a fall. Falls are common when you hike, but there is nothing more embarrassing than sliding down a steep hill on your butt with your shorts around your ankles, dragging a streamer of toilet paper. I assure you it will result in a whole new trail name. And as I mentioned earlier, if you attempt any of the techniques outside your reach of the toilet paper, you may find yourself hiking with only one sock.

Before any attempt to poop in the woods, however, there are some steps to take:

Find a suitable spot. Identifying animals by examining their poop may not be a hobby of yours now, but by the time you reach Maine, you will know enough different species using this method that you may be able to get a full scholarship at UMaine in their environmental studies program. Getting on all fours to determine what kind of animal you are sharing the trail with will actually be fun, until you notice what you thought was bear scat, was actually human due to the corn and pea remnants from a recent burrito.

Get away from the trail. Find the most discrete spot behind a bush, tree or rock, and then go a few yards further. Remember, with over three million people using the trail last year, you aren't the first person to find that spot. Being seen in that most compromising position is extremely uncomfortable, and no one can shake the image ounce it happens, but try not to bushwhack too far. Explaining to search and rescue that you got lost trying to find the perfect pooping spot is equally embarrassing!

Dig a hole. Six inches should do it. It doesn't have to be very wide either. With a little practice you will be able to hit your target with surprising accuracy. A good hole is the key to a sanitary forest. The Great Smokey Mountains National Forest has very few privies and therefore an area where "holding it until you get to the next shelter" isn't an option. In order to keep the bottom of everyone's shoes clean, we must all dig holes. A trowel is best but a stick can work, too. When in Pennsylvania, digging a hole can be impossible. When I find myself in a very rocky area, I simply pull a rock from the ground, use the hole and then place the rock back.

Prepare to wipe before you start. Hiking all day is hard on your legs. Don't put yourself through the agony of trying to find the end of the toilet paper while you are squatting over a hole with your legs trembling in pain. This is even harder when it is raining. This prep also frees up your hand to swat mosquitos or shield your face from passing hikers.

Leave No Trace. Upon completion, all paper products should be pushed into the hole and the hole covered back up. Once this is completed the worms can take over and the world can be a better place for it. The real nut eaters of the world will argue that leaving your poop and the TP in a hole isn't following the "Leave No Trace" motto. I say, when properly done, it is fine. Besides, if you think I'm hiking through the backcountry with my poop in a bag, you are nuts!

The common opinion of those who consider backcountry bowel movements a normal practice is that there are several preferred techniques utilized to accomplish this natural task. Here are my favorites:

Tree Hold Technique

This requires the aid of a sturdy tree, preferably six to ten inches in diameter. A dead tree is dangerous and may fall when you place your trust in it, possibly resulting in injury and rendering you unconscious in a most undignified position. Your hole should be dug 18 to 20 inches from the tree and the area around the hole should be cleared so there are no obstructions between your bottom and the hole. We don't want any blocked shots.

With these preparations made and toilet tissue placed in a convenient, easy-to-reach spot, you are ready to position yourself. Facing the tree, place your feet in a slightly widened stance so you are straddling the hole. The widened stance allows you to shift your weight from leg to leg during lengthy sessions. The ability to shift your weight is also helpful when you wipe. At this point it is time to pull your shorts down. This may feel uncomfortable at first but within a couple weeks it will be as normal as using your own bathroom.

Now, with your non-wiping hand, reach around the tree at waist level and using it for stability, squat. A full squat will naturally lift your heels off the ground and allow you to easily rest your quads on your calves. Surprisingly, you'll find this position moderately comfortable. While in this position you'll also be able to use both hands if you need to, or lean forward onto your knees to hide from curious hikers. Clean up is a breeze. All necessary paperwork can be performed

SAM "SAM I AM" DUCHARME

from the squatting position, or, if the legs begin to burn, you can straighten your legs and bow. The tree is used to hoist you back up to the standing position. It is especially crucial when you are on a hill with unstable footing, or when your legs fall asleep. This technique is favored by most hikers because of the stability the tree offers on all terrain, the availability of functional trees, and it is a must when your legs are wrecked.

Open Squat Technique

This method is the same as the Tree Hold, just without the tree. The practical use for this is that you can use it behind large cover like boulders, gas stations and dumpsters. Good balance is needed because it's difficult to stand after hiking twenty miles, making it slightly harder to rise from the squat. This limits the pooper to level ground unless you are on a sabbatical from the Cirque du Soleil. I was utilizing this technique in a relatively flat but stony area on a hillside when I lost my balance. To find stability, I grabbed a large boulder about the size of a keg of Budweiser. It instantly dislodged its fragile perch and slid down toward me threatening to crush me! Diving for my life, I escaped injury from the least expected place on the trail. Mosquitoes aren't the only hazards you face when you poop in the woods.

Horizontal Fallen-Tree Technique

Although seldom used, this may be the all-time favorite technique for hikers, hunters, campers, and those from the Northeast who just enjoying pooping outdoors. The reason it's not exclusively used is because you need almost perfect conditions. Those conditions include: a medium-size tree, approximately 30 inches in diameter; it must be no higher than 18 inches off the ground; and have 3g reception (reception optional).

All pre-poop preparations remain the same as the previous techniques; otherwise it's easier, more comfortable and relaxing. The idea, after dropping your shorts, is to scooch yourself against the log so it touches the back of your calves... and sit. This places your weight on the back of your quads. When done properly, your butt will extend out beyond the log allowing unobstructed evacuation. This can be trickier to hit your target so some skill is needed, but with the right tree, it's very comfortable. Leaning forward slightly leaves your hands free for that selfie and quick upload to social media. Using this weight-shift allows you to rest your elbows on your knees and catch up on the news, Facebook and texts... thus the reception. This is the only recommended technique where multiple people can utilize the same hole with ease. Some pre-planning is recommended.

This doesn't cover all techniques and methods. Sometimes you just have to drop your pack and dash into the woods and hope you get your knickers out of the way in time. (I lost my glasses during one of those episodes.) I also heard one hiker tell a story how in a desperate moment, he just grabbed a low hanging branch like he was learning to water ski, and "let her rip."

I hope this was helpful. The next time you hear someone say they pooped in the woods you will appreciate the process like a skilled karate move or beautiful yoga position. Once you are comfortable pooping in the woods you will find it is very efficient. The deep squat used is a natural position and is very beneficial in expediting the process thoroughly. It is also very sanitary. Privies and public restrooms can be a breeding ground for germs, and no one wants to catch the norovirus – acute gastroenteritis will drastically hinder your hiking. (Privies germy, woods clean.) Pooping in the woods is also extremely convenient. In the great outdoors, you don't have to look for a restroom, porta potty or truck stop. It also puts an end to transgender bathroom debates.

Yes, pooping in the woods can be awkward and uncomfortable if you aren't used to it. Practice and a plan helps, but sometimes it is just plain fun... to talk about.

Mak and Cheese

4

The Hikers

 The first few days were a real test for me physically and I had my moments of personal doubt. Unquestionably, the scenic views were becoming more impressive as well. The part of the trail I hadn't expected, however, was beginning to show itself. I had been so absorbed in my personal struggles to transform into a hiker that I hadn't seen the people who were going through their own transformations. It became very obvious that the people were going to be a large part of this hike.

I don't know if a few days on the trail constitutes a person as a hiker, but I was surrounded by a lot of people who were hikers in my eyes. Some of these hikers were starting to be a regular sight on the trail, especially at the water sources, mountaintops and scenic views. These places are a good place to sit and rest, snap a few pictures and eat a snack. Generally, hikers congregate here and it's where you get to know each other. These are the hikers in my "bubble." A bubble is the term used for the group of hikers that share the trail during the same timeframe. The timeframe isn't specific; it can be a three-day bubble or a two-week bubble. I left in mid-March along with many hikers; it was a big bubble. As the group progresses north, they spread out and the faster hikers break away creating a smaller bubble ahead of the big bubble. Get it? The mid-March bubble gave me my first taste of the kind of people hikers are.

The image many get when they think of a hiker is pretty standard: lean, tan, granola eating, bearded (men), pony tailed (women, or men) and earthy. Most of these traits are true, but they don't all start that way. Most are regular people who start out as the typical overweight American, soft from a life of conveniences. Surprisingly, even the young hikers fit this pre-hike description. Before you all get offended, let me remind you that this doesn't accurately describe those who live an active lifestyle of eating just enough to stay alive, running half marathons every weekend, and instruct spin classes 15 times a week. No, not you guys. You look fit when you start in Georgia. The rest of us, however, start off looking and smelling like regular people. Eventually, the beards, hairy legs and great physiques follow.

You know how when you are sitting in a diner having breakfast and two State Troopers are sitting in the next booth and how you try to listen in on the conversation? And how you can't understand them because it sounds like they are talking in code? "I had a code 10 on the big road and called for a hook." You don't know it is an accident on the interstate requiring a wrecker, because you don't speak trooper. Well, hikers have their own lingo, too. It took me a while, but bit by bit I learned ...

"Most hikers in my bubble were NoBo, but there were a few Flip-flop-pers. It was okay to YoGi as long as you don't ask. We all believed in MAGIC and ANGELS, but neither are found in huts. Blue Blazes were fine as long as they were less than "point-2," and Yellow Blazers

aren't thru-hiking. ZEROs and NEROs are good, but beware of getting sucked into the Vortex. Don't get caught calling Katahdin, Mt. Katahdin! It means The Greatest Mountain, so when you say Mt. Katahdin it is redundant." Copy that?

Hikers are free-spirited and spontaneous. I think it's a result of all the fresh air they are sucking in. Maybe it's knowing you don't have to go to work tomorrow. Whatever the common gene is among them, they know how to enjoy the things around them at any given moment. When it is a bridge, they may jump off it or just stare into the shimmering water below. At night it's the stars or a crackling campfire. When in town, it might be a hot shower at the YMCA or an all-you-can-eat buffet. Rain can be a bummer, but once you are wet, it's fun.

Most hikers like beer. Pabst Blue Ribbon is the unofficial hiker beer of the AT. When you are in the woods for several days at a time, sweating your body lean, you really want a beer. Even those people who don't regularly drink beer, enjoy the occasional beer when in a trail town. Those among us who like a beer will tell you the Pabst Brewing Company in Milwaukee, Wisconsin, has brought many hikers together around campfires, pavilions, trailheads and small town bars all along the trail. It serves the budget-minded hiker well.

Remarkably, I was surprised to see how many people smoke on the trail. I'm not judging, actually the opposite. First of all, I found it ironic that these young adults, whom I found to be so smart and articulate, smoked to begin with. After all, it is the 21st century and we all know how bad it is. Secondly, I didn't expect to see people out in the woods hiking all day, actually smoking. I hate to admit, I was a little jealous. I don't smoke at all and I could barely seem to get enough oxygen at times! Interestingly, most smokers buy the tobacco and roll their own cigs or "rollies." It is cheaper, easy to pack and there's no trash to throw out. I'm sure you would like to hear about all the pot on the trail, but I'm not going there. I don't care if you smoke pot or not. I will simply say that those who smoke pot as part of their lifestyle at home tend to smoke on the trail. I chew tobacco – who am I to say anything.

Another trait most of the hikers had was they are wicked smart, especially the younger crowd. I guess I expected intelligent conversation from the older and wiser hikers, but I hadn't given the younger hikers enough credit. They would easily go on about religion, politics, technology, legal matters, current issues and micro brews. It was refreshing to hear the youth of our country speaking so intelligently. Most of them wouldn't be able to drive a stick-shift, but they could tell you what was going on in the world of technology.

Every year there is a big hiker festival held in Damascus, Virginia. One of the most popular events during this weekend-long party is the talent show. Hundreds of people sit around the stage for an afternoon of songs, musicians, comedy sketches and poems. Throw a few jugglers, hoola-hoopers and burpers in and you have a show. The reason this is such a hit is because many of the hikers are very talented. A campfire turns into an event when a hiker brings a guitar. If the only song you ever heard played on a ukulele was by Tiny Tim, you are missing out. One night in Maine, while lying in my hammock, I could hear the music of a ukulele accompanied by a beautiful voice of a woman drifting through the dark like the smoke of a campfire. While she sang I didn't move a muscle, I wanted to hear every note. It was as beautiful as any of the sights I had seen during my journey. I never met the owner of the voice and that made the experience even more mystical. Thank you for that, whoever you are.

Hikers have talents that range from bar tricks (like darts) to equilibristics, as "Stache" would demonstrate with his Devil Sticks. "Easy

Strider" could be seen performing complex tricks with his yo-yo. There were a lot of musicians, too. Eventually, as the bubbles shift, you will get to hear a harmonica, flute or something with strings. If there is a piano to be found in town, it would be making music by an unshaved person, wearing worn hiking clothes and a dirty trucker hat.

Hygiene

As the trail grinds on and a hiker gets further from life's modern comforts, some changes begin to happen. Fight it as you may, hygiene begins to slide. This begins to be obvious by the time you reach the Smokey Mountains. In the Smokies you are mandated to use the shelters. Up to this point I was able to camp alone in the woods, free to strip naked every night and conduct my nightly ritual of taking a baby-wipe bath. I wouldn't call myself a germaphobe, but somewhere during my career within the prison walls, I became acutely aware of all the airborne and blood-borne pathogens that are out there waiting to come in. I'd call myself "germ conscious."

I was fastidious in my efforts to avoid the slightest contamination by bathing religiously. Foot fungus, Jock itch, norovirus, poison ivy, pink eye, ticks and anything else that can be avoided, discovered or eliminated with a nightly scrubbing, was getting my full attention. I quickly learned that not all hikers adopted my hygiene model. I would later learn that even with all my efforts, I had fallen well below the accepted hygiene level of most modern civilizations.

This pungent condition becomes part of life on the trail. Even when great lengths are taken to remain clean, you still stink. Your clothes remain dirty, sweat stained and wet for days. That goes the same for your pack, but even longer. Most hikers can't wait to wash their dirty hiking clothes when they get to a town. It is very common to see hikers wearing their rain gear in the grocery store while the rest of their clothes are running through the "Heavy" cycle at the laundry mat. The pack seldom gets the same attention. Even after a wash, hiking clothes still stink. It is just a fact.

Let's talk about the "Body" in body odor. As I mentioned before, hiking is hard. You sweat a lot. Now, surprisingly, sweat doesn't stink. Seriously. The smell comes from the bacteria that feed on fatty cells that used to be your love handles. They catch a ride out of the burning building with your sweat. The bacteria aren't harmful and are easily washed away with soap and water. Baby wipes work well, too. Basically, if you don't hunt these stinky little bacteria down, you will end up with foul smelling pits, groin and feet.

Stay with me now, this keeps getting better. The bacteria continue to multiply, getting stinkier, for about three weeks until it levels off. I'm not trying to suggest that any hikers actually go that long without bathing. Most of us don't. Let me try another route. When I was a kid I worked on a local farm. After a while I didn't smell the cow poop on my boots. The same thing applies to hikers. After a while you stop noticing how you smell. It wasn't until a year later when I was shuttling some "clean" hikers to the trail from Gatlinburg, Tennessee, that I realized just how bad we smelled. It was just like that feeling you get when you step inside grandma's closet – the smell transports you back to your childhood. For 15 miles, I was transported back to the trail.

I couldn't find an explanation on the Internet, so maybe no scientist has discovered this yet, but let me be the first to document a well-known fact among hikers. When your body has burned all the reserves within, after the love handles melt away, and when your beer-belly and butt have shrunk down to nothing, you start to emit a new odor. As you know, I'm no doctor. My expertise is in the inner workings of the American prison system and the criminals within. You may not think that is grounds to be a credible source to write about the human odor.

Well, I assure you that field has prepared me well. My exposure to the vast range of odors that the human body emits, unfortunately, renders me an expert. I also retired that career with an extremely acute sense of smell. Sometimes it can be a curse. I am particularly sensitive to foul odors like bad breath, body odor and human feces. This super-power comes in handy, however, when locating a dead mouse within the walls of my house.

This new odor emanating from the transformed hiker is easy to detect. You don't have to be an odoroligist to pick up on it. As far as I have seen, no one has died from it, although it has caused people to wish they hadn't picked up hitch-hikers. The odor is very ammonia like. It doesn't resemble typical body odor, athlete's foot or Jock itch. It is not limited to those common areas; it can be detected on the torso and back as well. When detected, the experts, usually the loved ones at home, prescribe more water intake, fearing dehydration. Although that may be sound advice, after hiking a thousand miles, all hikers are experts in hydration. No, it is the smell you get when there is no fuel left to burn. Your body is out of gas. You can no longer sustain your caloric deficiencies with your fat reserves. It is kind of like the propane tank right before you run out. It is telling you "Pay attention, you are running low."

I know that last part was fascinating, and the whole hygiene topic may be a turn off, but it is a part of the trail. Some hikers do their best to stay clean and others flat give up. I was determined to stay clean even if I had to carry packs of clean baby wipes in one bag and dirty ones in another. In Virginia I developed strained patellas. Your patella is basically your kneecap. Feeling like superman can cause you to over use your knees, especially when you descend mountains like a mogul skier. I decided to gut all of the nonessential weight in my pack to give my knees a chance to recover. One of the things I sent home was my deodorant. Within a week, my friend "Full Throttle," knowing my hygiene behaviors, eloquently brought to my attention that I no longer smelled fresh and clean. Despite my painful knees, I bought a travel size deodorant the next time I hit a town.

The whole hygiene issue even affected some hiker behavior. Fist bumps replaced handshakes. This wasn't a pop-culture thing; you just didn't want to shake hands with someone who may have been duct taping a blister or applying talc to jock itch. Those are just common activities in that world.

Body Changes

At this point my body began doing amazing things. It was metamorphosing into a hiker's body. Long-distance backpackers can burn between 5,000 to 6,000 calories a day. It is impossible to pack enough calories to replace what you use and it results in weight loss. For a guy like me who worked hard at maintaining size and weight by working out and eating lots of protein, I had a lot of weight that was better suited for wrestling with inmates rather than hiking up mountains. Eventually, my non-essential weight melted away. The fat was divided between being used as energy reserves within, and keeping a sporty shine and temperature regulation on the outside. By Pennsylvania I had lost over 50 pounds.

This is why when you think of a hiker, they are thin, lithe and stinky. In addition to the weight loss, I was fascinated with the metamorphosis my musculature was going through. I was getting T-Rex syndrome. The muscle mass from my arms and shoulders were shrinking and my back was becoming thin. My latissimus dorsi, deltoids, bicep and triceps muscles had shrunk down to the size they were in high school! My legs, which were always slightly above average in build, remained that way and even became more defined. I was amazed. My body was adapting to the task at hand.

This got me thinking: My body was changing similar to what a pregnant woman's body does. Now, before all you women stop here and use my book as toilet paper when you are pooping in the woods, I know I have no place talking about what it is like to be pregnant. I agree with you; I'm not trying to do that. I'm merely recognizing what an amazing thing the human body is. Look at the similarities. It is fascinating. Keep in mind, these similarities occur for different reasons, but you can't dispute the parallels:

- Almost immediately, hikers experience a **heightened sense of taste and smell.** I'm sure the hiker experiences the heavenly taste explosion of a supreme pizza because of their bland diet of almonds and Cliff Bars. Never the less, according to Parents.com, this is an early sensation those who are pregnant experience.
- Hikers find themselves **overjoyed one moment then stressed out the next.** This happens a lot when a hiker reaches a false summit. The joy in reaching the top is quickly changed to stress when he or she realizes there is still three hundred feet to go.
- **Exhaustion, nausea, vomiting, sore body, headaches and constipation.** Unlike a pregnant woman, a hiker doesn't have to wait a few weeks for these symptoms to occur. In my case, most of these symptoms occurred within the first few days. The intense change of physical activity, novice water usage skills, abrupt change of diet and poor conditioning made me a prime candidate for morning sickness.
- Within weeks I was **shopping for new clothes that fit.** For completely different reasons, I found my original clothes weren't fit-

ting. Like the women who were shopping at Nordstrom, I was both proud and excited about my changing body.

- I was experiencing *food cravings.* I found myself reciting one of Dr. Seuss's familiar books while I hiked: "I will eat them in a boat, and I would eat them with a goat..." Now you know how I was given the trail name "Sam I Am."

- A hiker's body *craves more calories.* This goes along with the last similarity, and although no hiker would turn down a pickle or bowl of ice-cream, the truth is that the body is screaming for more food because it needs the calories to accomplish the task it has been handed – just like the expecting mother.

- *Frequent urination.* With the exception of "Mrs. Fancy" from Germany, who conceived while in the Shenandoah's, to the joy of her and her husband "Mr. Fancy," most hikers don't try to thru-hike pregnant. Therefore, we aren't experiencing expanded uteruses. We are experiencing increased water intake resulting in frequent urination. A stretch? Maybe, but similar just the same. Incidentally, Mr. and Mrs. Fancy eventually had a daughter and named her Virginia.

- I certainly wasn't becoming voluptuous, but there was no arguing that I was *experiencing body changes.*

- Toward the end of my hike, specifically the back side of New Hampshire and through Maine, I was finding my *emotions were all over the map.* Each time I began thinking of my boys or pictured myself on top of Katahdin, I would become emotional. Missing my boys was always just under the surface.

- This similarity is so real it is almost spooky. *If you make it to Week 14, your chances of making it to the end increase substantially.* I'm certainly not going to make light of this one. In both cases this is a point where it becomes safer to start thinking of the future and thus allows you to enjoy the journey even more.

Do you see? I could go on about hair changes (mostly on legs and faces), decreased libido, fatigue, breathlessness, etc. The one last thing worth mentioning is Due Date. By the time the due date starts to get close, both the pregnant woman and the tattered hiker is ready for the big day. It has been a long journey for both. They are tired, uncomfortable and eager to complete their own journey. Unfortunately, the due date is rarely correct. Despite all the planning and calculating, it is not an exact science. The extreme differences happen upon completing this journey – the work has just begun for the Bearer of life; the hiker is finished.

Guns and Safety

As you can see, hikers are an interesting bunch. It doesn't take long to start acting like a family. Some people might think we are taking a risk heading out into the woods with so many people around. We all watch the news and we know the world has become a dangerous place. People commonly ask me if I went alone and if I brought a gun. As I mentioned earlier, I did go alone. As for carrying a firearm, I took the advice of the REI specialist and left it home. Not necessarily because I was smart enough about pack weight though. I am a proud gun-toting American. I am trained. I was a firearms instructor. I've been exposed to critical situations and I am able to make sound decisions under pressure. As long as I am able to, I will legally carry a firearm. Everyone is safer when there are competent people with sound judgment carrying firearms. The key word is "legally." There are several resources covering the legal possession of a firearm when in national parks, federal parks, crossing state lines, national scenic byways, etc. I couldn't find a definitive answer, so I left it locked up in my safe in Connecticut.

I've met some bad people during my career. I am aware of the dangers that are out there. I am glad to say that I did not find myself in any sort of danger, of the human kind, anywhere on the trail. That doesn't mean there weren't a few sketchy people out there. There were. The AT affords free lodging, fresh water, and plenty of nice people to beg from, making it an attractive option for a few waiting to take advantage. They don't last long. That kind of reputation travels fast. Besides, it takes a lot of effort to climb mountains and after a few mountains, they are done.

Any threat, if you want to narrow it down, is most likely to occur near a town. The trail does have some bloody history, but if you are smart, these higher risk areas are easy to avoid. I made it a point to camp a mile from a road crossing when it was possible. It is tempting to camp close to town to resupply first thing in the morning, but I would stop early and camp away from these spots. Having raised boys, I learned that one boy equals one brain. Two boys equal half a brain, and so on. When you add a 30 pack of beer to the equation, the numbers go exponentially down. It's best to avoid a situation before it is a situation. Judging from the beer cans found near the trailheads, they look like a convenient place for the locals to party. I also figured the partiers would party close to the road because it was a lot of work to hike that far with beer. The camps with the most incidents were the ones in town where a pavilion or designated area within the town was made available to hikers. I avoided most of these as well. I also didn't see myself as a soft target either. Why mess with me when there were younger smaller people to trouble? As a rule though, most communities were extremely welcoming and gracious to hikers and rarely did I hear of any trouble at all.

Another factor that adds to the safety is numbers. You are never alone. When a sketchy person is acting rude or disruptive, the hikers join together. Usually the person is told to move on by the majority and that is enough. Sometimes they don't get it. When this happens, police are notified and they gather descriptions of the person. Eventually they make an arrest at a road crossing. They are usually hit with a disorderly conduct or disturbing the peace charge and you don't hear from him again. The numbers factor into trail help, too. Even during long lapses of solitude, if you were to injure yourself, another hiker will be by soon. On the same note, you don't have to worry about being kidnapped from your campsite at night. You never have to camp alone. I chose to do this because I like to, but the shelters are usually occupied, and there are almost always good camping spots in those immediate areas. You do have a good chance of being robbed though... by mice.

Blood Mountain

5

Mountain Crossings

 After four days, I was on top of the world. I was still suffering from poor conditioning, which would last about a month. It was the month from hell, as I refer to it. Despite that, on Day 4 I had already hiked three days longer than any previous hike in my life. I was starting to get familiar with some of the hikers in my bubble, and the anxiety of the first few days was fading. Day 4 involved a climb up Blood Mountain where a beautiful clear day offered a picturesque mountaintop view. Many of the hikers I had been leap-frogging for the last few days were enjoying the sunshine and taking in the splendor that can only be enjoyed from the top of a mountain. The sun had warmed the rocky top and the wind was blocked by the highest boulders allowing us to remove our lightweight jackets and bask in our first major climb. I moved away from the summit, took my boots and socks off and dozed. I like naps, but I don't like the idea of sleeping when I could be doing cool stuff. So, long ago, I decided naps were okay as long as I take them in cool places. This qualified.

I was beginning to understand the magic of hiking. I loved mountaintops before I started this hike. I remember driving my '65 Mustang up to New Hampshire when I was sixteen and visiting my childhood buddy who moved away. I never passed the chance to hike up a mountain, especially if it had a fire tower. I chuckle looking at the pictures of my skinny, teen-aged self, standing on top of Mt. Monadnock in New Hampshire. I wore corduroys and work boots, before water bottles and without a pack, shirt, food or anything else for that matter. The only thing I carried was a little plastic camera. (Clearly there was no REI in my area at the time to teach me the way.)

Back then I loved skiing and although I loved skiing at our local hill in Woodstock, I would travel up to the ski areas in Vermont and New Hampshire as often as I could. Riding up the lifts was as fun as skiing back down. I just love the mountains. I would work as a ski instructor at OHOHO Ski Area, save my money and spent it up north in ski country. Those day hikes and lift rides were great, but looking back at my youthful energy, it was all so easy.

Now, as I was taking in this mountaintop experience, I was euphoric. I got my first taste of really earning it. The last few days of struggling up mountains to find no views, only to descend and repeat was torture, sheer torture. I was sore, exhausted, disappointed at myself for coming so unprepared, and was getting no gratification for my hard work. Today was my big payoff. As I looked over at the distant mountains and the deep valleys with the sun shining down and the happy chatter of my fellow hikers, I was moved. I was so happy to be right where I was, lying on that rock slab, resting in the sun, thankful to be alive. I missed my boys; it was the kind of place they would have loved.

I dozed for about an hour not wanting to move on, but after putting my socks and boots back on I headed down the other side. Moun-

Day Four

tain Crossings was ahead and with any luck, this would be my first sign of civilization I would find since I started, and I could use a shower. I hiked without resting; gravity would be my friend as I descended the long switchbacks that Georgia is famous for. I would look to my right and the great mountain would be like a wall, so close I could reach out with my hiking pole and touch it. To my left I could see the long dark trail zigzagging down the mountain. After each turn it seemed like I was making no progress, stuck in a repeating motion and seemingly no closer to the bottom.

Somewhere in between the switchbacks, I heard someone closing in fast. It was Colt 45 and he was on a mission. Mountain Crossings was a hiker-friendly stop situated in a gap between two mountains. Many hikers, after spending the last four days hiking, switch up gear, send over-packed items home, and rent a cabin for the night. There is also a nearby town where, if you can arrange transportation, you can get a taste of restaurant food. Colt 45's mission was to get down the mountain and secure a cabin for the night. It was first-come-first-serve, and he was determined to watch some college basketball.

This wasn't the first time he passed me. In fact, he passed me once a day for four days. Every night his father, Carusoe, and he would agree on a camping spot for the following day. In the morning Carusoe would head out with the other hikers, and Colt 45 slept until ten or so. Being a young collegiate soccer player, he was in great physical condition and a very fast hiker. Sometimes after lunch he would catch up to his Dad, confirm the camp location and continue on. The locations weren't complicated, usually they were shelters. Colt 45 would get there very early, filter a gallon of water from the water source (his part of their arrangement), and sleep the rest of the afternoon. When his dad arrived later he would get up, eat supper (cooked by dad, his part of the deal), and go back to bed. The duo were well known for this symbiotic father/son relationship. Besides, we all got passed by Colt 45 each day.

On the way by he told me his Dad wanted him to ask me if I was interested in splitting the cabin three-ways. I agreed and he was gone. The weather was taking a turn for the worst and by the time I made it to the Crossings, I was wet, cold and tired. When I arrived, I walked right past Colt 45 because I didn't recognize him freshly showered, changed and without the skull face mask he hiked with. Thankfully, he stopped me and showed me to the cabin. A while later Carusoe came in wetter, also sore and tired. It was great to have a hot shower and to be out of the cold rain.

It continued to rain and the forecast for the next day was bad, so we decided to enjoy ourselves and visit with some of the other hikers.

There was a small general store where we could congregate with the others while we all waited for our clothes to be washed. We sat in rocking chairs dressed in our rain gear, while a crackling fire slowly warmed the chill from our tired bodies. There were ten of us, all familiar faces from different times within the last four days. This was the first time we all sat together. It was like the first days of school. The friendships formed that night turned into my very first "Trail Family." A trail family is core of friendships and contacts that can rely on one another for information, splitting motel rooms, encouragement, companionship, help and transportation. We decided to exercise our new benefits by hiring a shuttle into town for supper and splitting the fee ten ways. Before we got in the van, we got the driver to take pictures of our group. He took ten pictures with ten phones. You will meet most of them before you finish this book.

I stared out the van window as we drove through the Georgia mountains wondering if I was looking toward the trail. Already the mountains looked different. I wasn't ready to start hiking again, not yet. Just looking at them brought thoughts of short breath, weak legs and stumbling feet. The van was comfortable. I would enjoy this meal, a warm bed and dry clothes, and I wouldn't think about hiking in the rain tomorrow. The driver navigated around a traffic circle with a monument in it the middle. It was a typical southern town surrounded with old red-brick buildings. I could picture the horse and buggies that used these same roads before Henry Ford flooded them with cars.

We all agreed on Italian. My mouth watered just thinking of spaghetti and meatballs! It had only been five days without "real" food and I missed it. We went to a fancy place with two forks and two spoons on the side of the plates, and pictures of the Coliseum and "Venecia" on the walls. We were a little out of place, but we acted dig-

My original trail family

nified... until the food came. Clearly, I wasn't the only person among us who missed real food. It got very quiet when the food came out. All you could hear was silverware clinking on plates. We must have looked like a pack of hyenas feeding on carrion.

That is the day I fell in love. It was an affair I had right up to the Mason Dixon line. My mistress: Sweet Tea. It isn't a trail name of a woman on the trail. I mean actual sweet tea. My northern taste buds had never danced with such sweet nectar! It was like drinking a romantic melody. I was hooked. Oh, the spaghetti and meatballs were good, too.

Riding back to the cabin was quiet. The van swayed on the winding road and the engine was loud as it labored up the mountains. The dark rainy night offered little to look at, and the few homes we passed were blurred from the wet windows. It was a good night to sleep under the roof of a cabin. We tipped the shuttle driver who seemed pleased, and we all headed to our little cabins with full bellies.

As I lay on top of the bed in my sleeping bag (I never sleep in motel linen... too germy), I wondered if this was what it would be like sharing lodging and eating at restaurants every week or so? It seemed okay. Maybe I'll give it another week... besides I could use some more sweet tea. I was in the loft only a few feet from the ceiling listening to the pouring rain when I fell asleep. Every now and then I heard Colt 45, down stairs, cheer for some team or other.

The next day was a washout. The rain continued coming down and the forecast called for no let up throughout the day. The thought of hiking all day in it was depressing. As new hikers we hadn't become accustom to being miserable yet, and I was easily talked into taking my first "ZERO." A ZERO is a term hikers use to describe a day off – zero miles. We hung our damp gear from the rafters, watched TV and shook down our packs. A "shakedown" is when you take an inventory of your gear and shave extra weight by eliminating unused gear. The weight we shaved was replaced with the weight we added by replenishing our food for the next stage of the hike. This routine would repeat itself for the entire trip. You would be light going into a town and be heavy leaving. It was hard to believe that I had only hiked 31 miles... 2,157 to go.

That group in the picture would be one of my favorites when I got home to Connecticut six months later. Of the ten, only two of us finished. To this day I've kept in contact with all of them, five of which are now close friends.

6

Hiking with a Pilgrim

 Back at that Italian restaurant, I shared a table with three hikers: "Bean Counter," the accountant from Louisiana; "How Far," the brother in law of "Bean Counter;" and "Dusty Pilgrim" from Plymouth, Massachusetts. Together, they were known on the trail as "The Three Amigos." All four of us were retired, and were considered "Old Guys" among the younger hikers. Whatever. Dusty met Bean Counter and How Far on the trail and hiked with them since Day 1. They got along fine, shared stories and shared campsites. I would see the threesome several times a day, passing each other during rests and enjoying views together as we discovered them. I think it was Bean Counter who gave me my trail name, and Dusty Pilgrim who notified me. Apparently, this "naming" happened without me present. It's an exciting thing when you get your trail name.

Two days after leaving the cabins at Neel Gap, I was summiting Rocky Mountain about 25 miles away. I saw Dusty Pilgrim sitting on a rock tending to some blisters on his feet. His tent was set and he was looking pretty relaxed, so I stopped to chat. He was in a great camping spot on the very top of the mountain. The site was covered with short grass, had a stone circle for a campfire and perfect trees for hammocking. The mature trees were oak and the perimeter of the site was surrounded with mixed hardwood brush and saplings. This time of the year you could see through the trees, in a few weeks it would be thick with leaves. The east side of the mountain dropped right off, as did the west. I might get to see a sunrise yet. I set my hammock, took my BWB (baby-wipe bath) and joined Dusty for supper. It was still early and it was a beautiful evening to camp. The sky was clear, there wasn't any wind, and wearing my long johns, I was comfortable.

I didn't know it at the time, but after camping with this 60-year-old retired fire fighter from Massachusetts, we would spend the next 364 miles hiking together.

Bean Counter, being an accountant and a details-guy, was on a strict itinerary and in Dusty's attempt to keep up he had developed severe blisters on his right foot. If you have hiked, you know how much of a hindrance a blister can be. Dusty, having spent his career rescuing people, knew a thing or two about first aid. He treated his foot as we enjoyed the late afternoon and got to know each better. It wasn't until two nights later that I would see his foot. When I did, I couldn't believe how severe it was.

We hiked two full days through a 25 mile stretch taking us through Indian Grave Gap, Tray Gap, Wolfpen Gap, Steeltrap Gap, Sassafras Gap, Addis Gap, Deep Gap and Moreland Gap. That is a lot of gaps. If you remember, gaps are the low spots between mountains. That means his foot was doing a lot of work in that condition. He didn't complain once. Eventually, we split up while I side-tripped to the post office and we met up again in a hostel later that night, unplanned. We decided not to take anytime off the trail, just sleep indoors, have our clothes washed, take a shower and head back out after breakfast. That is when I saw his foot. It was bad.

The skin between his toes blistered and peeled off, leaving the sensitive pink skin underneath exposed. The constant movement of his foot wasn't giving it a chance to heal and it was very red and aggravated. Dusty would carefully clean it, apply an ointment and tape it so he could continue hiking. His boots were chaffing the backs of his calves as well. Between the two hot spots on his legs and his painful right foot, I don't know how he continued on. He did continue though, tending to his foot when we stopped, and experimenting with his boots to try to relieve the rubbing on the backs of his legs. He cut his padding off his boots, then improvised new padding, taped his legs and anything he could think of to keep hiking. Eventually we crossed into North Carolina. In Dusty's words, "We are out of Georgia Jurisdiction!" 2,110 miles to go.

We both had hiked 78 miles in ten days. Not a very impressive feat in the hiking world. Crossing out of Georgia and into North Carolina had an incredible effect on our spirit though. The state line was just a tree with a small worn sign nailed to it. The state names weren't even spelled out; only the abbreviations are on it: NC/GA. I felt like I was up on Blood Mountain again. Finally, I could check a state off. A mental victory. We camped near an old twisted tree above Bly Gap and the weather began to turn. Despite the rain and fog, we were thrilled to be in North Carolina!

We hiked on together for the next three days. We had a lot in common and we didn't have any problem jumping from one conversation to the next. Neither of us had been hikers before so most of our conversation was limited to the downhills. Dusty is a very tall man, career fire fighter, and former Army Ranger. One tough son of a gun. He packed everything he could find in his basement and carried it on his back. All those years pulling hoses up stairwells had prepared him well. I loved hearing the stories of his rescues. I thought if I had a heart attack climbing out of one of these gaps, I might have a chance. He has a "wickid" Boston accent which made me feel right at home. Being from Northeast Connecticut, we drink "Beeahs" at "Baahs," too. Before I got too attached to my new buddy, I had to make sure he wasn't a Yankees fan, which would have been a deal breaker. At the mere mention of the word, he almost laid a beatin' on me! We were good. See, New England is funny. Three states touch New York: Connecticut, Massachusetts and Vermont. For some dumbassed reason, some New England residents claim loyalty to New York teams. I don't get it if you want to root for New York, move there.

The miles became a little easier as we talked about familiar things like the New England Patriots and Boston Bruins, Cape Cod, the Berkshires and New Hampshire. Outdoor activities like camping, fishing and hunting kept us talking for hours. Our former careers had placed us each in some dramatic situations and we told some of those stories, too. That would require another book. It also helped that we shared a similar sense of humor, the kind of edgy humor that helped us deal with a stressful career.

Dusty was the Clint Eastwood of the trail. He is tall and confident, and a little intimidating because of his serious expression. But really, he was a marshmallow, always stopping to meet new hikers and carrying on with the three icebreakers. But he did have a short fuse. One night while stopped at the only shelter on the trail that was completely empty, Dusty gave me a refresher course on some of the most popular and long forgotten swear combinations I'd heard since retiring from the prison.

When I began hiking with Dusty, I started camping closer to the shelters because he liked sleeping in them. I would usually camp some

Dusty – the Clint Eastwood of the trail

distance down the trail and he and I would meet up again in the morning. This shelter had an excellent hilltop campsite only about 100 yards away, so I camped up there. Sometime past midnight I heard Dusty swearing up a storm and it sounded like he was in a fight! Naturally I rushed to my new buddy's assistance, after all, he was like my very own walking CPR machine if I went down.

When I got to the shelter in my bare feet, I saw Dusty sitting up in his sleeping bag flailing away with his trekking pole, like a ninja, smashing the sleeping platform! His head light was flashing back and forth so fast I couldn't see his attacker. Eventually he stopped, huffing and puffing and visibly pissed off. When I asked him if he was having night terrors, he looked at me like I was the crazy one! He explained that the mice were literally chewing on his sleeping bag, and when he turned on his light, two of them were playing tug of war with his chamois! I asked him if he thought he might have been overreacting He told me it had been going on since he tried to go to sleep six hours ago. He had had enough. It didn't stop after his Bruce Lee imitation either. He just became so tired he finally fell asleep. When he woke up in the morning, his towel was chewed to shreds right where he was sleeping. Vermin, another reason I sleep away from shelters.

As tough as he was, Dusty had a weakness... rain. He didn't like hiking in it or camping in it. This aversion to rain exposed a chink in his armor and I used it often during our friendly banter. I teased him about how he hiked with one eye on the trail and the other toward the sky. By the time we were in Tennessee, he was practically a meteorologist. When the clouds became too dark for his liking, he would stop at the nearest shelter and call it a day. It drove me nuts!

On a particularly rainy day, just north of Big Butt Mountain, we slid down to the Flint Mountain shelter where Dusty had enough hiking in the rain. Although it was early in the afternoon and we had plenty of hiking light, Dusty wasn't moving. I could tell, because he was stripping off his wet clothes and blowing up his sleeping pad. Reluctantly, I conceded rather than move on without my new buddy. I waited for the rain to let up so I could set up my hammock in the area. The shelter quickly filled up and the weather was continuing to get worse. Against my camping strategy, I decided to sleep in the shelter. Shelter sizes vary. This one was rated to eight people, which means four or five section-hikers, or twelve or thirteen thru-hikers. We had a full house of fifteen. "Giggles" was sleeping on the picnic table which was pulled inside the shelter. Or was it "Shits?" I get them two mixed up.

The inside of the shelter looked like the New Orleans REI store after hurricane Katrina. There were dripping packs and hiking clothes hanging from all the rafters, and clotheslines strung throughout. While everyone was claiming spaces for their wet clothes, I claimed an end spot near the wall to sleep. This would have been my all-time worst night on the trail if it wasn't for Dusty.

The shelter was packed to twice the capacity, and there was no room to move. The floor was dirt and with the heavy rains and dripping hikers, mud. The space between the sleeping platform and the open side of the shelter had three rows of clotheslines full of wet clothes, and the place smelled awful! Normally the sound of rain on the roof was music to my ears, but on this afternoon it was very loud causing the hikers to raise their voices until the combination grew to a cacophony of hikers trying to compete with Mother Nature.

My choice of sleeping space hadn't proved to be as good as I had hoped. It was just past midafternoon, and even though the hanging clothes blocked out much of the dreary light from outside, it would still be several hours until hiker midnight. I decided to strip off my wet clothes, climb into my sleeping bag and tune out the commotion of the shelter with some music from my iPod. As you may or may not know, you don't need a packable air mattress when sleeping in a hammock. When you are sleeping on a platform made with old worn boards however, they come in handy. I didn't have one. Maybe it was the hard uneven boards or the way my head was three inches lower than my feet, whatever it was though, I was uncomfortable. I looked over at Dusty who had been tucked in and snoring for an hour, and I wanted to pop his sleeping pad! I was a little grouchy, but the storm was a doozy and I was glad I wasn't out in it.

Dark thick clouds accompany storms like this one, and it was dark a little earlier than normal. The hikers were cramming into their places for the night. I switched my head around and pointed it toward the open side of the shelter and hoped the blood would return to my feet.

Just as I was starting to drift off, a commotion came from the gauntlet of hanging packs and wet clothes. It was a late hiker announcing himself with a spot light on his head as he forced himself through the rows of clotheslines with his pack on. Let's just call him "Don Knotts."

Having spent every night comfortably camped alone in my hammock and not being trained in shelter life, I made a rookie mistake. As all the other hikers lay in the previously quiet shelter listening to the torrent of water pounding the roof, I lifted my head and looked at Don Knotts. He instantly stepped up to me and started talking. He asked if he could squeeze in. He was very pleased with the progress he made despite the weather and it clearly invigorated him into wanting to give me all the details. He must have taken my silence as permission, because he talked away as he dripped all over me, removing his pack, shoes and rain gear. Following his elaborate meal and all the clatter that accompanied it, Don Knotts preceded to do the only thing that would prove more inconsiderate than arriving at a shelter at nine p.m. and keeping everyone up while he cooked supper – he stood four inches from my head and undressed.

Having worked in prisons for twenty years, I've seen my share of nuts and butts, but this was a little too close for comfort, even for me. I guessed the last time he saw a baby wipe was when he visited his great grandchild. Meanwhile, everyone else continued to pretend to sleep. After a couple minutes of playing dodge ball, I elected to sleep with my head on the downhill side. I tried not to touch the walls because of the water flowing down the stones in little rivulets. "Don Knotts" noticed the small space between me and the wall and asked if I minded if he placed his gear there. I was ready to scream.

Don Knotts was starting to irritate some of the fake-sleepers because he made no attempt to be quiet. He rattled his cook pot like he was calling cats to supper, and shined his light like he was looking for a lost child. Shouts of "LIGHT!" were repeated several times and he would calmly reply, "Sorry." When he finally wedged himself between me and the next hiker, who was a very good fake-sleeper, I turned my iPod back on and waited for all the blood to flow back into my head. Don Knotts immediately began to snore one of those loud, open mouthed snores that driving rain nor AC/DC could drown out.

Everyone who sleeps in shelters has had their own Don Knotts. As ridiculous as this story sounds, every word is true, except his name. I already knew I wasn't going to get any sleep. I was uncomfortable, laying at an incline, and my patients were stretched thin. It was that exact moment that I was resigned to just lying there until sun up. I could do that. That was also the same exact moment when all the rain that had fallen in the last six hours, caused the wooden roof reach maximum saturation.

The good news was the leak wasn't directly over me; it was further up the roof. The bad news was, as it ran down the inside of the roof to the back wall, the water hit a nail perfectly positioned four feet over the bridge of my nose. At that point it released its grip on the porous wood and followed the path of least resistance, streaming onto my face. If I had been lying there with my headlamp on, staring at the ceiling I would have seen it, but as I lay there doing the exact same thing in the pitch dark, I did not expect the stream of water to land in both eyes! I let out some of Dusty's creative vocabulary combinations. I remained awake until day break, but I sat against the back wall in my sleeping bag with knees pulled close under a rain poncho that said "Gatlinburg."

The saving grace of this miserable night came around 3:30 a.m. I was sitting and over concentrating on the rhythmic drip hitting my tourist poncho, when Dusty sat up and yelled! He only used three words, but the effect was shocking. "DO YOU MIND!" Now my hear-

ing isn't very good, I had an iPod on playing "Sunglasses at Night" for the sixth time that night, and I was mentally impaired from the Chinese water torture, but I reacted just like everyone else in that shelter; I nearly jumped out of my sleeping bag! No one was faking their sleep judging from their reactions. Everyone, including Giggles on the picnic table, shot into the sitting position confused and frightened into wake.

Dusty's light was on and it looked like an episode of The Walking Dead. When enough lights came on to see him, a very pissed off Dusty sat with his blaze orange knit hat sitting crooked on his head. His light was shining on "Crackers," who was sitting up, frozen with his hand in a trail mix bag. In his hard Boston accent and low gravelly voice Dusty said to Crackers, "Weeya tryin' to sleep in heaah!" Dusty must have startled Crackers, too, judging by all the raisins, M&Ms

and nuts all over his sleeping bag. He slowly lowered his crinkly bag trying to be quiet and softly replied, "I was hungry." I laughed that laugh you laugh, when just as you think you are done laughing, you start laughing all over again.

"Can you hear me now?"

7

Staying Connected

 Over the years hiking the AT has gotten easier. The trail has become eroded in places, making it somewhat trickier, like in the Smokies where you are literally hiking in a trench, or in Vermont where decades of hikers have pounded the soil into a muddy mess when it rains. But overall, the journey has become easier. When Grandma Gatewood hiked the trail in 1955 she carried a sack over her shoulder and wore canvas sneakers. The gear has come a long way and there have been a lot of trail improvements. Bridges and stairs have been built and improved, drainage has been specifically and discreetly engineered from end to end, and technology has enabled us to stay connected.

When my buddy "Beerman" thru-hiked the trail for the first time in 1978, he didn't have the luxury of smart phones, social media, GPS, instant weather reports or baby wipes! His idea of an upload was hoisting a big framed pack onto his back. A lot had changed between that hike and his second thru-hike where we met and became friends. I imagine it was nice to hike unencumbered, without texts, emails and phone calls. I'm sure he spent more time looking at the views, rather than looking for a signal. Time has indeed changed since then and I'm not going to try to tell you the differences. Beerman is writing that book. If you make it to the end of this book, look for that one.

YouTube & Internet

With millions of people using the trail, you probably won't get lonely for company, but being away from family and friends for six months is hard. With the advent of cellular communication, at least you can stay connected. Most large phone providers have pretty good service; a couple of those are very good. I was able to make a call or shoot a text out on about two-thirds of the trail. The tops of mountains were pretty reliable as were areas near trail towns, but the low areas like the gaps, were definitely dead spots. The more remote stretches between communities were unreliable and most shelters, due to their location in low areas near water, were sketchy as well.

I'm not a techno-wiz, so I won't bore you with all that stuff. I will, however, tell you what a huge impact these modern conveniences had on my thru-hike. No amount of technology will make the hiking easier. Mountains are mountains. Going up is hard work and going down is no picnic either. There is no app to change that. What it does do is it gives you the ability to look at your son's face thousands of miles away, have a conversation, and tell him "I love you" whenever you miss him. In my case I had two boys, and they were far away. We would do this often. The easiest route over a mountain is any one you take following a conversation with a loved one.

Most of the people in your life had never known the size and scope of the AT before you started talking about it. Now that you quit your job, announced on Facebook that you were heading out to attempt a thru-hike and you are storing nuts like a squirrel, they want to follow along on your progress. Whether they want to follow along to see the beautiful pictures and live vicariously through you, or they just want to know if they win the office pool when you drop out, they want you to stay connected. The information superhighway gives us lots of ways to do it. Social media is as much a part of the AT now as it

Beerman

is in any high school in America. There are the occasional unconnected people out there still, but you'll never hear from them... get it?

As I alluded to earlier, I did a lot of research by watching YouTube. I also felt some emptiness planning an adventure without my two favorite adventurers, my sons. We spent almost two decades exploring, road-tripping and enjoying life with the zest one looks at the last day of school. Our "mystery trips" would sometimes lead us into the heart of the Adirondacks, shooting at deer camp or flipping rocks in a local stream. It wasn't beyond us to spend a couple hours playing "Deer Hunter" (a video game) in an interstate rest area. We were inseparable. YouTube gave me a media option to share my trip with my boys and bring them along every step of the way. I'd watched a YouTube personality, "loner2012AT," as he documented his journey, and I was fascinated. I knew this would be the way to share my journey with my boys.

I certainly wasn't tech-savvy, so I YouTubed that, too. My very first video proved my technical shortcomings; I posted it with my head cut off! I wasn't worried though, the only people likely to see it were my kids and they would probably laugh at my old-school ignorance. That was wrong, too. I learned that there are thousands of people watching this type of thing. I thought of my mother and sister watching. Maybe my nieces and nephews would see it, too. I had to pay attention. My brother makes his living editing, and I didn't want to embarrass him professionally. My challenge was to figure out how to record, take pictures, add text and edit it all together. The hardest part, however, was my language. I speak English, no problem there. The problem was that, after dealing with inmates for so long, I cursed... a lot. I didn't want to be recording and have to throw the video out because I cursed. I also wanted to be completely candid. It took a few tries and a few clips never made it to the public, but before long I was rolling a series of videos documenting my attempt to thru-hike the AT. My format would be... no second takes.

Being unique was going to be hard. I feared the "cookie cutter" approach and didn't want to make hours of "walking-with-a-camera-in-my-face" videos. When I saw the amount of people on the trail, I found my answer: Show the trail and its beauty, the hardships and especially the people. Within days I was starting a project that would bring the trail and its people to homes and offices around the world. It connected me to many fellow hikers and was the source of fun, stress and unexpected support from hikers and non-hikers worldwide. Yes, this prison guard was an unlikely ambassador for the AT, but I was doing my best to represent it – and its culture – as I lived it. I did it all with my phone.

The recording was the fun part, most of the time. When you are in the forest with all these fun, smart, determined people, it is easy to find good material. Most hikers gladly put up with me when I stuck my camera in their face and asked them "What's your name, and where're you from?" At the very least they had a solid alibi for that moment in time. When I gave them the opportunity to say hi to someone, they would light up and say, "Hi Mom!" I tried to keep it light and happy, and for 2,189 miles I was diligent, writing names of those I met, specific details I wanted to share, and thanking the people who were reaching out to me from cyberspace. I was well-known in my bubble and some of my fellow hikers were becoming regulars. It was turning out to be a reality show. I would gather the material all week and put it on YouTube on the weekend.

Before you upload a video it had to be edited. All the videos, still pictures and text had to be joined into one longer video. I did this in my hammock at the end of the week. I would review my daily material, deleting duplicate pictures, clips with swears and clips that didn't turn out good. I did keep some clips that seemed shaky or hectic though. I couldn't find it in my heart to cut a nice hiker out. I felt like I was going to give him/her bad karma. I was working hard to keep my "G" rating. Who knows, maybe I would even have grandchildren watching it someday?

With all of the movie making, I was running into problems. I could only load these videos when I was in town. Maybe there was another way, but with my file sizes and data usage, it was out of my league. Now before you turn to the next chapter because I'm crossing into the "What the heck is he talking about" area, understand that I didn't know any of this stuff and now I was trying to figure it out on the trail. I expected to have some trouble with blisters and rain but I wasn't expecting trouble with data storage, battery usage, SD cards, upload speeds and all those things; until now they never applied to me. I didn't even know what 3g meant. (Actually, I still don't.)

I tried to put up a new video each weekend. Sometimes I would have to do it early or late depending on where I was. I would leave the trail, find a public library and use one of their public computers. After several weeks it felt like I was hiking from library to library! Being a self-proclaimed library geek, I found sitting there waiting for a video to upload a nice retreat from the grind of the trail. I was also amazed at some of these beautiful new libraries. The staff was used to hikers coming in to check their emails and read periodicals, and I found most to be pleasant and helpful. The modern libraries with their fast internet speeds had me back on the trail fast. As for the ones competing for the title of "Oldest Library on the AT," I'd spend up to six hours waiting for a video to load!

When I couldn't get to a library, I would stay at a cheap motel or hostel with an internet connection and post a video there. These often have slow internet speeds or bad Wi-Fi connections, so I began avoiding them and springing for the more expensive motels and hotels. I spent many nights sitting in the hotel lobbies using their one, germ-infested computer, keeping the third-shift desk employee company while my video loaded.

This was becoming a huge burden to me and it was affecting my trip. The time off-trail was starting to add up and I was constantly struggling to juggle data storage on my phone. I was finally starting to understand what all the phone commercials were talking about on TV. Early on, I had to leave Dusty on the trail when I went into town, and then chase him for a couple days, only to leave him again the following weekend. The hotels were costing me money I hadn't planned on, too. In Atkins Virginia, I split a room with "Forrest" in one of the dumpiest motels on the trail. I had to leave my phone in the lobby until 2 a.m. waiting for the slow internet to load, leaving me waiting outside. Luckily for me, the rooms were so disgusting that I didn't have to wait alone. After purchasing beer at the gas station, BeerMan, Drop Bear, Rugeru, Palimino, Colt 45, Carusoe, Forrest and I, pulled an all-nighter sitting outside. These people were my current bubble, and familiar personalities on my most current videos. It is a fond trail memory and comes up often when talking in that circle.

I continued being diligent into Tennessee, but I was starting to think it was too big of a project to continue. I would dig deep, turn the camera on and smile as I brought the trail developments, black bears and new hikers from the trail to the living rooms. I wasn't even halfway and I hadn't figured out how to continue putting up videos and still make it to Maine before winter. I would hike all week with new hikers, and then leave them to go into town. The next week would be a repeat. Dusty had gone home just before Virginia to attend his son's college graduation, and I had been hiking with new bubbles each week since. Up to this point my motivation was showing my boys, but I was even talking myself out of that. I was ready to quit the project.

That was about the time two things happened. The first thing was exciting: Viewers were starting to reach out to me. One viewer, Mike from Arizona, offered to send me a package of supplies. I was touched by his offer. I thanked him but didn't accept. I was a retired adult and didn't want to take advantage. He left the option open. I was telling the story to another hiker and I was surprised with her response. She told me to accept the offer because the people watching like the idea of being involved in my hike. She also said some people are just nice people who feel good helping others. I hadn't looked at it that way, so I decided to let Mike send the box. Before I could message him, however, he beat me to the punch. His message informed me that a box was already waiting for me in Damascus, Virginia, and they were holding it until I arrived. Mike and his wife Ashley sent me so much food that I was able to share Oreos, squeezy cheese and Triscuits with several hiker who were also in Damascus that night. (Mike also sent me several nips of Jack Daniels. I had to hide them, though, because the hostel I was staying at had a strict no-alcohol policy.)

The activity on my videos was beginning to become noteworthy. Even my boys were beginning to sound impressed. (Those of you with kids know how hard it is to impress them!) The activity was also in the form of trail support. People were writing me notes of encouragement and inspiration, and offered to pick me up on the trail, feed me and give me a bed to sleep in. I was amazed for the hundredth time in two months! People weren't just watching, they were hiking the trail with me! Over a thousand people were watching the videos each week, sending me messages of support, asking questions and thanking me. I was pumped!

This support carried me through Virginia. But by the time I hit Pennsylvania I was worn out. I went through a tough stretch and had lost a lot of weight. My energy was low and I was hiking some short days. The thought of spending more time off the trail to load a video was starting to feel like a bad idea.

During this time, I decided to hitch into a town for some breakfast. I was standing on the side of the road Near Waynesboro, Pennsylvania, with my thumb out. It was one of those days when my thumb just wasn't producing a ride. After about fifty cars blew by, I was ready to give up and continue hiking. Just before I gave up, another car came down the hill. This car slowed down very rapidly, swerving over just as it passed me. I almost jumped in the bushes! The driver's door flew open and the driver briskly began walking toward me. I had been walking 2.5 mph for a while now, and all this seemed to be happening fast. That's when this happy looking man pointed at me and asked, "Sam I Am?" I was relieved that he wasn't pointing a gun, but I know for certain I never met him before. I answered that I was and inquired if we knew each other. He replied, "I know you, I've watched all of your videos!" He introduced himself as "Tada." He watched all the YouTube hikers every year and that he (especially) enjoyed my videos. He also told me to get in the car and tell him where I wanted to go.

On my way for some hot coffee and breakfast, Tada gave me the second bit of advice that motivated me to see my video project to the end of the trail. He simply advised me to continue. "The worst thing about watching videos each year," he explained, "was that by the time they get to PA the videos just stop." He never knows if the hiker quit or finished without recording it. Either way, it was disappointing that he would never know. Here was a man I had never met, telling me he felt as though he knew me, asking me to finish what I started. His advice came at the right time. If I hadn't met him, he wouldn't have seen a video from me that Sunday night. We shot a quick clip and I went in for coffee.

Trail Angel Sheepdog

8

Magic and Angels

 Prior to beginning this hike, I planned to do it alone. I pre-packed supplies to be sent and relied on a friend to drop them in the mail, but other than that I was thinking I could do the rest on my own. That was wrong. I learned that something as routine as going into a town for supplies can be impossible if you don't get help. I also learned that there were people ready to help. Those people are called Trail Angels. The help they offer is called Trail Magic.

I found this phenomenon within a few days of my hike. I was stumbling into a gap, dreading the climb out, when I hiked up to a group of people sitting around in soccer mom chairs. Some were clearly hikers and others seemed like normal folks, just having a picnic. Those normal folks invited me to sit for a spell, and kindly offered me a soda. The timing was good; I was pretty tired from all the walking and I didn't pass up the chance to sit down. I accepted a soda, after all I didn't want to be rude, and enjoyed some friendly conversation. They offered me snacks and clean water, but not knowing these people, I didn't want to take their picnic food. I thought it was neat that they chose this place to picnic. It was like they were set up early for a parade, only the parade was the hikers. After, when I mentioned what had just happened to some other hikers, I was told that I had just received "Trail Magic."

These nice people weren't hikers. The only reason they were there was to show some kindness, offer us a chair to rest in and share their food and water. I surround myself with great people, so I'm no stranger to kindness, but when you experience an unexpected act of kindness from a stranger, it is very humbling. It took a while for it to sink in.

Dusty and I had hiked a stretch when we dropped into a gap in the middle of nowhere. The trail guide I carried said "dirt road." This was common. Most dirt road crossings were eventless and momentary, like stepping over a rock. This road, to our surprise, had a group of college students from Young Harris College, and they were members of "The Trail Magic Club." They had homemade snacks, coffee, soda, and they even had a tarp set up next to a fire to take a break out of the rain and warm up. We were delighted to see these young kids, roughly our own kids' ages, seeking out strangers, just to offer them a snack. It wasn't the coffee or the fire that warmed us, it was their kindness. Dusty and I had spent our careers being the go-to people, offering services that help and protect others. Now here we were – on the other end. It was an unfamiliar position to be in for both of us.

Another time, I had been hiking in bad weather for days when I found myself at Newfound Gap on the NC/TN border. I wanted to get to Gatlinburg to put up a video, dry out, drink some sweet tea and eat a hamburger. When I looked at the sign, it said it was 15 miles away. It was 4 p.m. and it looked like going into town wasn't going to be an option. Disappointed, I was getting ready to hike on and forget the whole idea. That is when a woman approached me. I was just sitting there on a rock, away from all the tourists, a little bummed out because I had just hiked four days through the Great Smoky Mountains National Park (GSMNP) and due to the rain, sleet and fog, I hadn't seen any views. I'd been looking forward to this section. I knew it would be very high in elevation and dramatically beautiful. I was lucky to see some wildlife, but the mud-slicked trails and cold wind-swept mountaintops were exhausting. I admit, the natural forces of Mother Nature continued to astonish me, but I was looking forward to a pit-stop in Gatlinburg.

"Are you a thru-hiker?" an attractive young woman asked as she walked through the grass approaching me like I was a lost puppy. "Not yet," I said. (That response had become my standard. A true thru-hiker is someone who has already completed the hike, not someone who is attempting a thru-hike. I didn't want to jinx myself, so I never called myself a thru-hiker.) She asked if I was going into town and if I wanted a ride! Her boyfriend and she were heading that way and I was welcome to join them. I gladly accepted, and down the beautiful winding roads of GSMNP we went. We stopped a few times to snap pictures and pet horses like friends on a road trip together. I was conscious of my muddy, stinky body and they assured me they stunk, too, from their hike. All I could smell from them though was shampoo and scented dryer sheets. They were being nice. When we arrived in town they asked where I was going and I said anywhere was fine, that I was going to find a cheap hotel. When Christine and Greg, who were vacationing from Michigan, pulled into a hotel to drop me off, they offered to pay for my room! Their generosity was so touching. I was speechless. I respectfully declined their offer, explaining that their offer to drive me to town and spending time with them was incredible, and that I wouldn't accept more.

These acts of kindness continued for the length of the trail. In the south, the Bible Belt, it was common to receive trail magic from the local church groups. They would cook burgers and dogs, or leave a cache of cold drinks and snacks in a cooler. One church in North Carolina held a pancake breakfast every day for three weeks during the hiker season. They ask only that you come hungry. The different churches never pushed their religion on us, they made themselves available for spiritual support if asked, but they let their kindness be their testimony. The church presence in the form of trail magic was so strong, I found myself changing my denomination three times a week!

Few things can lighten your pack like hearing that trail magic awaits ahead. The thought of a hot dog or a cold drink inspired me to pick up my pace on many occasions. In contrast, arriving to a cooler that holds empty cans and empty doughnut boxes is devastating. One afternoon, Dusty and I pushed for four miles at a trot because we were told that pulled pork was being served. When we arrived, we saw the truck driving away as we came out of the woods. "I really wanted an apple," Dusty said in a soft disappointed voice. As if on cue, it began to rain at that moment.

This whole concept of trail magic had an incredible effect on hikers. The positive energy of the Trail Angels could turn a frustrating stretch of trail into a trail party. That's exactly what happened when I was delighted to find tents erected in Rockfish Gap. The rain had been relentless and that section of trail had a lot of field walking. When you walk along fields, the long wet grass saturate you from the waist down and the constant rain from above insure that you continue to stay wet. This day was bubble-shoe wet; that means, you are so wet, your shoes make bubbles when you walk. My raincoat had long stopped being effective; in fact, all it was doing was filtering the water! When I stepped over the wooden guard rail, I saw two tents near the trailhead. Afraid to get my hopes up, I approached with caution hoping it wasn't a mirage. Until I was called to join in, I was a drenched, tired, miserable hiker. Within minutes I was surrounded by happy Trail Angels and giggling hikers. After they fed me and gave me a place to rest, they also arranged transportation to town where I spent the night. The last thing they did when I was dropped off at a motel was give me a list of other Trail Angels in case I needed anything else while I was in town. That is where I met "Pepper." Pepper was on the list, and when I asked her for a ride back to the trail, she picked me up and drove me back. It was only about ten miles back to the AT, but during that time her positive attitude, willingness to help strangers and genuine kindness will always be a fond memory of my hike. We remain friends to this day. It was fun texting back and forth as her Cubs won the World Series.

Trail Angels usually tend to be hiking enthusiasts. They hike, are former thru-hikers, like the idea of hiking, or just like hikers. Many non-hikers become Trail Angels without knowing it, by picking up a hitchhiker. The trips into towns are critical for hikers. We can only pack so much food so we have to go off-trail to re-supply. Ask any long distance backpacker and they will tell you they hate off-trail miles. 12 trail miles plus 4 off-trail miles equals 12 miles. Off-trail miles suck. To avoid the off-trail miles, we hitch hike. In most trail communities, they know who we are and why we are hitching. It is pretty easy to get a hitch. Some people pick up hikers all summer long and some are just driving through the area and pick up a hiker to be nice. In both cases they are Trail Angels. The driver gets a quick story of an active adventure in progress and the hiker gets a lift to Dollar General. Keep in mind, this is not always a treat for the driver as it may take days for the car to return to its normal smell! I was always so thankful for those hitches because I was aware that my appearance had gone from normal: "He looks safe" to: "He's a hiker, let's pick him up" to: "Homeless." I have been picked up by a church lady, a stoner, a soccer mom, town drunk, dog lovers, contractors, a teacher and a former gang banger. Normally I am very weary of strangers; there are many felons doing time for committing awful crimes. But if the choice is to risk kidnapping or doing off-trail miles, I'm taking the ride.

"Stache," "Rapunzel," "Huckleberry Thug" and I, were hiking near Harpers Ferry, West Virginia, when we met up with "Happy." Happy got a shuttle north and was hiking south at the time, and he informed us that there was "hot" trail magic about four miles ahead. We picked up the pace so we wouldn't miss out. When we arrived at the trailhead, there was no one around. When you have gutted out all the things that occupy your mind, you find yourself overly focused on food. This food-focus borders on obsession. Arriving at trail magic too late is mentally deflating. Our disappointment was quickly replaced by hope, however, when we spotted a grill. It was all alone where we imagined trail magic would have been held. We were elated to find the grill still warm and the charcoal still burning. When we lifted the cover we could hardly believe our eyes. On the grill, were several pieces of chicken and one hot dog. The Trail Angels left it for us! We fist-bumped all around, (hikers don't touch hands which works for me,) and ate all the chicken. Food drunk, we sat on the grass basking in our good fortune and timing, when a van pulled in. A woman got out of the van and approached us. Thinking she was our Angel we all greeted her and got up, preparing to thank her for the chicken. She politely excused herself as she worked her way around us to the grill where she explained she left it to cool off. Instantly we all realized that we had just eaten someone's food! As our eyes darted around to each other, we felt like thieves who were about to get caught. Sheepishly, we explained what happened at which she graciously forgave us. Looking back, I realize that even if we found that grill in the top of a tree, we would have thought it was left there for us.

My journey was dotted throughout with these unexpected acts of kindness. They slowly peeled the layers of dirt a callous world can leave behind. When I started the trail, I was like a dirty onion, grimy from years of dealing with untrustworthy people and the stains left behind. I was beginning to have renewed faith in people. The occasional reminder that there are still good people out there was really refreshing, it was like peeling the dirty layers off.

At first, when I experienced trail magic I would try to pay the Angels. When they wouldn't take it, I would leave money on the seat of their car. Eventually, I learned that these Angels really just did it because they love people! Many of them would tell me how they admired anyone who would attempt a thru-hike, and while they would talk, I'd be thinking how I admired what they were doing. For me, it was like being in fantasy land, or the Twilight Zone.

I became friends with "Full Throttle" and "Grasshopper," section-hikers who started out at Springer at the same time I did. They are two of the original ten in my trail family. We all hiked the trail and experienced the same trail magic. When they went home we kept in touch and they followed my progress on YouTube. When I reached Pennsylvania, they surprised me by coming to the trail and conducting trail magic as I came by. All the hikers in my bubble benefited that day as Full Throttle and Grasshopper knew just what to bring. That magic was especially sweet.

Sometimes I received trail magic when I least expected it. Without any notice coming down the trail, I was stopped on several occasions and asked if I was a thru-hiker. When I explained my standard answer "Not yet," I was offered a variety of nice magic. Naturally it was always food. I still couldn't get over how thoughtful people were. Offerings were made miles from roads by day-hikers who planned ahead by bringing extra to hand out: a turkey sandwich in Vermont, peaches and brownies in Massachusetts, soda and candy in Connecticut, dehydrated fruit in Georgia, and summer sausage in New Hampshire! Yes, I remember all of them. When two little children you meet on the trail can't open the Tupperware fast enough to hand you a brownie, it melts your heart and sticks with you. In this case their Mom had taken them for a hike to find thru-hikers. I sat right down and ate it in front of them with full fanfare, humming with every bite. They were tickled pink that they made me so happy. After all, they "had been looking for a thru-hiker all day!"

I could go on about how "Maxfactor," from West Virginia, scouted for hikers all day and took us to his condo(s) near the Shenandoah's, fed us, re-supplied us and offered to let us stay at the golf/ski resort as long as we wanted. He bought two condos and hosted up to ten hikers a night. The resort was huge, complete with full amenities, and Maxfactor was an incredible host. I could also mention Meg from Worcester, Massachusetts, who sent cookies from her cookie baking club. Another pair of Trail Angels in Virginia, whose son previously thru-hiked had their own names: "Mama Goat" and "Grumpy Goat." So as you can see, this outpouring of kindness goes on and on. As I experienced more trail magic, and met more Trail Angels, my world was becoming a better, kinder place. After receiving trail magic, I would continue hiking astounded by the warmhearted, generous people I was meeting, and they were complete strangers! As I hiked on, I could feel another layer peel off.

You will hear more stories of trail magic as you continue up the trail with me because it had a huge presence during my hike. You will also see that fellow hikers can be Trail Angels, too.

Grasshopper and Full Throttle

"Warm and Toasty," a fellow hiker, treated me to trail magic more than once. Leapfrogging her cars from south to north, she would hike south passing me nearly every day. By the time we got to Maine we were close friends. She drove me to town in one state and back to the trail in another. Each time she used a different car.

Somewhere in the Tennessee mountains, I received a message from "Sheepdog" and her husband "Diesel." They are real-deal hikers. She is a K-9 officer and he is a paramedic, a big paramedic. They are both professional people-helpers. Sheepdogs were used in the 19th century as drovers. Drovers are dogs that help protect cattle and sheep from predators, much like her job as a police K-9 officer. When they aren't hiking, preparing for their next hike, or thinking of hiking, Sheepdog and her K-9 partner can be found out in her community protecting her flock. Diesel and their other dog, "Angus the Adventure Dog," are her hiking companions, and they can be found section-hiking the AT.

Sheepdog and Diesel had seen a few of my videos and saw that I was getting close to where they lived and reached out to me. Because of their love of the trail and our K-9 connection, she offered to help with any trail needs I might have as I passed through. They also invited me into their home for a rest, shower and a comfy bed. I thankfully acknowledged her message but told them I was fine and that I'd keep her number if I ran into any problems. K-9 officers are like that; it's like a fraternity.

Shortly after that correspondence, the word on the trail was that a nasty storm was heading our way. At first, I didn't pay much attention and I hiked on. Dusty, however, didn't like the reports that were reaching us through the other hikers. High winds, heavy rain and danger from falling limbs had him looking skyward like a pilot's spouse looking for a late plane. Right on schedule, the weather began to turn and I called Sheepdog to see if she had an accurate update on the storm. "It's a good time to get off the trail," she said. "Where are you?" We were camped for the night and not far from a road in another gap, of course, and she told us to be out at the road by 7 a.m., and she would be there to pick us up. Sheepdog was right on time and she brought us back to civilization where we were hosted at their home. They let us hang our wet gear in the garage, washed our dirty clothes and gave us each a guest room to use. The weather system missed us, but we were treated to a day of sightseeing and relaxation while we got to know these great people. It was a rare day off, filled with pasta supper, a hockey playoff game, a warm night in a clean bed, a big breakfast and two bona-fide Angels; it was a good ZERO indeed. *Another layer gone...*

The Sawtooth Mountains in the GSMNP

9

Through the Smokies

Before my trip into Gatlinburg, Tennessee, I lost Dusty. In the GSMNP in an effort to minimize the hiker impact on the forest, camping is not permitted. Shelters are available, and unless they are full, you must sleep in one. When we arrived at 5:00 p.m., the shelter was full. The wind and rain hadn't given us a break all day and we were looking forward to stopping. During the winter months, the park installs tarps to close the open side of the shelters for added protection from the wind and snow. When we lifted the tarp and stepped in, the hikers were already laying in their sleeping bags trying to warm up and protecting their spots. No one answered Dusty when he greeted everyone. It was a combination of section-hikers and thru-hikers and there was an obvious tension in the air. I think Dusty liked the quiet and instead of asking, he told a couple of hikers to make room. I had hiked with him long enough to know he wasn't sleeping outside in his tent. I decided that I didn't like the energy in that shelter so I moved on. There was another shelter in six miles and I would go there.

I know it seems like many of my stories occur during inclement weather – and that would be an excellent observation. In this case, my decision to move on during these conditions caused me to become separated from Dusty for four days. I headed out knowing it was going to be dark soon. I was able to cross over Thunderhead Mountain before dark and I stopped to soak in some of Mother Nature's awesomeness. There is a small space on the summit where the trail opens into a bare gravel area, surrounded by thin alpine vegetation. Rocks protrude from the gravel offering a seat after the 19 mile climb. This open ground was an anomaly and I was sure it was because of the view. If I wanted to see it though, I'd have to Google it, because it was socked in clouds. At 5,500 feet above sea level, the relentless wind was blowing the clouds into the side of the mountain, forcing them to flow up and over the ridge top to escape. The brush was alive as they raked the white ghosts as they flew by.

I couldn't stay long, daylight was quickly fading and the temperature was dropping. I hiked the last couple miles in "rain dark;" the kind of dark where the rain and fog seem to suck the light out of your headlamp. I didn't rush. The rocks were slippery and the rain turned from light and intermittent to steady. By the time I arrived at the next shelter it was 8:45 p.m. I wasn't planning to disturb the hikers within due to the time, so I found two trees in the area and decided to hang my rig there. My tarp sounded like small arms fire as it snapped in the strong wind, and I took twice as long setting up due to my numb hands. I wondered if I had made a mistake. I risked hiking at night, during a storm, and for what? I was camping outside anyway.

By the time I got set up, I was wet and frozen. I was shaking, my teeth were chattering and my frustration was bordering on panic. I wanted to climb into my sleeping bag with my wet clothes on. Luckily, I recognized my irrational thinking as dangerous and I stripped my wet clothes off. I forced myself to bear the cold, while I pulled my dry long johns and socks onto my wet body. I climbed into my sleeping bag and began feeling better immediately. Under the protection of a thin tarp my stress level began to drop as my body temperature rose.

The rain kept up through the night and other than a brief run to the little boy's tree, I didn't come out from under my tarp until it was time to pack it up and move out. If you've hiked in the rain, you already know it is an exercise in determination. I believe the expression "puts a damper on it" came from a hiker. It was probably coined while the wet clothes from the previous day were wrung out and put back on. There is cold when it is in the 20s. And then there are days that feel cold because of the wind. The coldest days, however, are the wet windy days. I woke to temperatures near 40, but the rain and wind made it feel much worse. I had just come down from the north where the temperatures were below freezing for most of the winter and yet, I was struggling to keep warm in what would equate to Indian summer at home!

For the next two days I hiked on, and eventually made it to New-found Gap where I would spend the night in Gatlinburg. The next morning I found a ride back up the mountain and continued past my first sign for Katahdin. It said 1,972 miles to go! Until I saw that sign, I was feeling pretty good about myself. I had hiked 200 miles, my legs were getting stronger, I was losing some weight, and I was in my third state. Seeing that sign made me realize the size and scale of the task I was attempting. I wasn't yet convinced that I could finish. Thankfully, the sun was out and I still had thirty miles remaining in the GSMNP. I was told the Charles Bunion viewpoint was spectacular so that was my next stop. I tried not to think of the mileage.

On the way, I saw a young boy, roughly 10 years old, sitting on a rock, crying. Nearby were a couple of men and another youth look-

ing at the view and taking a rest. I stopped to say hi to the boy who was struggling, and perhaps encourage him. While I spoke with the unhappy hiker, one of the adults asked me if I was "Sam Ducharme?" That's when I met Rich. (His real name on and off the trail.) He explained that he recognized my voice from my videos! Rich was on vacation from the USAF and had been conducting trail magic for the Warrior Expeditions group. They are a group of military Veterans who were hiking the AT. After treating the Warrior Expeditions group to trail magic, he was enjoying the trail with his hiking buddies, "Big" and "Small." Rich and I hiked together until lunchtime and I decided to join them at a shelter for lunch.

Most shelters are set off the trail as conditions dictate for wind protection, space, etc. This one was no exception; it was 30 yards or so off with a trail leading to it. When I approached the shelter I noticed lots of gear hung and lying out, drying in the sun. Sitting with his back to me, waiting for his gear to dry, was Dusty! He passed through Newfound Gap while I was in Gatlinburg! I was back with my hiking buddy! I rarely stopped at shelters; in fact, I avoided them. On this day, I was going to have lunch with Rich; otherwise, I would have hiked past and missed Dusty. "The trail will provide." That saying is common among hikers when things like that happen. It is almost like the trail is a living thing watching out for hikers. If the boy wasn't sobbing on the side of the trail, I wouldn't have spoken to him, Rich wouldn't have heard my voice, and I wouldn't have stopped to have lunch at the shelter. I would kid Dusty by saying, "We are meant to hike together."

That's exactly what we did, slowly grinding out miles on sections with rugged names like "Sawteeth," "Snake Den Ridge," "Max Patch," "Hot Springs," "Big Butt" and "Devil's Creek." The gaps were endless, each having equally inviting names, most having to do with devils or bears. And my favorite: "Deep Gap." (There is more than one with that name.) Having a hiking companion made the miles a little more bearable. My legs were getting stronger and my stamina was beginning to build, but I still hated the climbs. Dusty and I would put our conversations on hold when we climbed and resume on the ridgetops and through the forests. Occasionally we would camp together between shelters but most nights I'd leave him at a shelter and I would camp alone along the trail and wait for him the next morning. He would update me on the trail gossip he learned at the shelter and then we would resume discussing the problems of the universe or take turns telling a tale from our past. Before long we hiked another 150 miles and we found ourselves sitting with several other hikers at the end of the day at a shelter six miles before Erwin, Tennessee.

I felt pretty good that evening and decided to push on without Dusty. The added miles would bring me closer to town and I thought it would be nice to pop out of the woods early enough to have breakfast in the morning. Somewhere within the first mile I had an encounter with a "root fairy." According to Carusoe, root fairies appear when you are tired, careless or both, taking the opportunity to snag your foot when you least expect it. I was tired and careless, eager to push toward town, when I tripped. I had been hiking faster than the normal pace Dusty and I kept, when my toe hooked on a root. The jolt shook me to a stop, redirecting my momentum, and threw me off the right side of the trail. In an instant I was crashing down an embankment trying to pick a safe route through the rhododendron. I soon realized that picking a safe route wasn't within my powers, and I desperately began clawing at the barky branches as I tumbled through them! Half-way through my second somersault, I came to a stop on my back with my head pointing downhill and my face looking skyward! The rhodo-dendrons proved to be my savior after all. The last bush refused to let me pass and held me like a giant spider web holds a moth.

It was the kind of fall you hope no one saw, but then again, it was such an epic fail you hoped someone captured it on video so you might win an episode of "America's Funniest Home Videos." I began assessing myself for injuries and a possible route back up to the trail I had just debarked from. I felt fine other than a few abrasions, but I'd have to get out of the bushes to find my way back up to the trail. This "downward turtle" position is a most awkward position to recover from. I was tangled in such a way that I wasn't touching the ground and the branches within reach weren't strong enough to pull myself upright. I felt like a turtle on its shell. I couldn't roll right or left. I was stuck, upside down, on my back, 10 feet from the trail. The good news was that at the very least, Dusty would be coming by in the morning. He'd know what to do.

I rolled and kicked like a horse scratching its back in a pasture until the branches and twigs cracked and bent. I slowly worked myself to the ground, resting on my pack. I managed to wiggle myself into a pushup position but standing would be impossible with my pack on, so I unclipped my waist belt. Gravity, doing what it does, shifted the pack from being securely around my waist to securely around the back of my head! This was turning into an exercise in humility! I managed to slide my pack off, perform a clumsy otter-slide out of the bushes and regain my composure. Within minutes I circumnavigated the life-saving bush and climbed back up to the trail.

An incident like that takes a few minutes to recover from and while I was sitting on the uphill side of the trail doing just that, "Easy-Go" and "Not-a-Bear" arrived. Easy-Go took one look at me and asked, "What happened to you?" Pointing at the small root in the trail, I simply replied, "I tripped." He took one look at the damaged bushes and disturbed hillside and encouraged me to "take a few more minutes" before I moved on. I must have been a sight because they both took a break and helped me brush the dirt and leaves off, while rounding up my poles, water bottle and hat.

We hiked on as a trio and arrived in Erwin, Tennessee, before dark. We went to a hostel and for ten bucks they allowed me to hang my hammock wherever I could find a spot. They had a common area outside with a small pavilion which had a movie scheduled for later. To make things better, a cooler full of beer was dropped off by a local trail angel. We had a pretty good turnout thanks to the beer. I don't remember the name of the movie, something about a professional bowler dude, but I remember the fun we had, laughing and talking late into the night. We covered a vast variety of topics but surprisingly, hiking never came up. One by one the beer was consumed, and before long the tired hikers retreated to their bunks or tents, which were set around the property. I had reconnoitered and decided to hang my hammock on the porch under the gazebo where the movie was played. The owner's wife told me it would be okay, as long as I got up early. I waited for all the hikers to go to bed and hung right next to a sign that said: "No sleeping on porch," Technically, I wasn't on the porch.

Erwin wasn't one of those must-stop towns on the AT. It is geographically a long narrow town with Interstate 26 bordering one side. The locals depend on this route to travel across town to the various eating establishments like Choo Café, China Kitchen and Hawg N Dawg. It is easily navigated by car but renders the hikers dependent for transportation. The post office isn't very convenient either, but you can rent a bike if you feel like peddling. The town boasts that they held the only elephant hanging in history in 1916. That's right, you read it correctly: Execution of an elephant by hanging. I haven't googled it, however, so I'm not sure that record still stands.

I wasn't the only hiker planning on a hot breakfast the next morning. The hostel offered to shuttle us to the local gas station where we could sit and drink coffee over a hot meal, so we gathered like a bunch of kids waiting for the school bus. There were 25 of us, or so, most of whom I knew like "Bison," "Day Late," "Bookworm," "Miami Vice" and "Fiddlehead." There were several hikers I met for the first time waiting as well and who would become well known to me as my journey continued: "Beerman," "Lean To," "Red Hot" and the original "Sam I Am." She claimed the "original" status because of her prior thru-hiking experience, and graciously shared her trail name with me. (When she wasn't around, I'd claim the "original" status.) The 25 of us crammed into a van with 14 seats and we headed to town. Rolling down Interstate 26 we endured strangers sitting on laps, elbows in faces and that familiar smell that we were all becoming accustomed to, just for a few eggs, bacon and hot coffee.

We were all happy – despite the long wait, a grumpy driver and cramped conditions. Three hours later we were back at the hostel wondering where we might go for lunch. By that time Dusty and several other hikers had arrived. They had their hopes of going into town to eat, so those of us who crammed in for breakfast, stayed back and let the late arrivals enjoy the shuttle experience. Later we would all cram in again and go to a different eatery where the hostel owners sat like bus drivers at Burger King, enjoying their free meals in exchange for the load of patrons. It wasn't a particularly good restaurant; one I wouldn't have gone to pre-trip, but one is not picky when a hot meal is only available once or twice a week.

Despite the transportation challenges, Erwin was a good place for a ZERO due to the long stretch of trail that preceded it, so Dusty and I decided to stay the following night. We lingered the next morning, repeated the morning shuttle to breakfast, and then headed back out on the trail. The sun was shining, we had full bellies and full packs thanks to a trip to Walmart, and we were in good spirits. We would hike another seven days, camping and talking the miles away. We even stopped at a hiker haven called Mountain Harbour, where we camped and had a huge breakfast the following morning. This place was known to have the biggest and best breakfast on the trail, and we agreed that their reputation, thus far, was well founded. This would be our last off-trail stop together because Dusty had to go home.

On Day 47 of my hike, after hiking for a month and a half, I found myself hiking alone again. Dusty Pilgrim had gone home to attend his son Nick's graduation from UMass. I would feel his absence immediately because I soon hiked past Laurel Falls, which I knew, he would love followed by an eighteen-hundred foot climb, which I knew he would hate. He planned to return to the trail following Nick's graduation. We planned to meet further up the trail and we would continue north. Following our summit of Katahdin, we would travel back to his unhiked section and we would hike it together. "The best laid plans of mice and men often go awry." This would prove to be the case.

Shenandoah National Park

10

Virginia is Not Flat

Hiking alone on the AT is a misnomer. There is always someone nearby. Hiking without a hiking partner is what I was doing. There is a difference. When you have a partner you have someone to share your experiences with – the views, wildlife encounters, weather challenges and ZEROs. I found myself missing the companionship I shared with Dusty, and in turn, the miles became longer. I would see a dark cloud and think, "Dusty would be freaking out over that one." Within a day and a half I crossed into Virginia, State #4, and I didn't have Dusty with me to fist bump. I snapped a quick selfie next to the Tennessee/Virginia sign and moved on.

Up to this point, it was a well-known fact that Virginia was the state to make up any lost time, and increase your daily mile average. The long climbs and high elevations are over for a while, the bad weather with snow and cold temps is a thing of the past... and the trail flattens out. Approximately 3.5 miles past the Virginia state line, in Damascus, as I lay on a hard wooden bunk in a church hostel, I savored my progress and looked forward to the easy hiking ahead. I should have been looking at my trail guide. The very next day, when hiking out of Damascus, near Rte. 58, there is a bridge. Following that bridge and continuing for the next 20 miles, the trail gains 2,000 feet of elevation! For those of you who might be thinking 2,000 feet isn't so bad, think about it this way: it is 185 stories. The Empire State Building is 102 stories. Now, add 83 stories and build a 20-mile ramp from Staten Island to the top of the new and improved Empire State Building. This climb took one long day. I was rewarded with a beautiful mountaintop sunset and camped nearby. "Jeopardy," who was camped in the same area, surprised me with a can of beer! I gladly carried that empty can for the next three days.

Virginia is the longest state along the AT. A thru-hiker travels over 500 miles in this state alone – or about one-forth of the entire trail. Believe me when I tell you: It is not flat! You won't find names on every mountain and it isn't uncommon to find gaps at 3,500 feet, but I found my mileage increase. I went from days of 10 to 13 miles increase to 18 to 21 miles during this stretch. It wasn't the terrain; it was my physical conditioning. Over the last 450 miles my legs had become stronger, I had dropped 20 pounds and learned to pack and hike more efficiently. I was turning into a real long-distance backpacker.

I was sharing the trail with an interesting group of people like "Philco" and "Forrest," "Rugaru" and "Palimino," "Beerman" and "Drop Bear," "Old Eagle Scout," and "Walnut." These hikers would drift in and out of my world at any given time. Sometimes we would hike several hours together, other times a day or two. We might not see each other for days and then meet at a hostel or trailside motel. Bit by bit we would build friendships and make memories. Imagine, wherever you are, whatever new town you find yourself in, you bumped into friends. They were at the restaurants, the laundry mat, grocery stores and the post office. These people add to my growing "trail family," the closet friends within my hiking community.

Sick and Injured on the Trail

Virginia held some drama – and doubt for me. I was dealing with physical challenges as well as gear issues. A few days before crossing into Virginia, I developed a noticeable cough. Like any man in America, I ignored it until it developed into full-blown upper respiratory infection. For the record, it took around 240 miles. By then, I was plagued with a constant cough and chest congestion. My high daily mileage was shrinking. The mildest uphill climbs would throw me into a coughing fit slowing my pace again. To compensate for my slow pace, I would hike later into the evening. Camping near anyone would've been rude, so I avoided that. Sharing lodging would have been worse, so that was out of the question as well. My attempts to get a prescription from my doctor in Connecticut were denied (you know how that goes), and I could no longer keep hiking because my chest was so racked from hacking. This would be my first real scare threatening my ability to finish my thru-hike. I decided to go to a walk-in clinic in Bland, Virginia. Unfortunately, the only one available there was twenty miles away and I'd have to log some off-trail miles.

Remember the expression The trail will provide? This is another example. There are Trail Angels, who as you know offer assistance without charge. Shuttle drivers, however, offer assistance for a fee. On this day, Bubba, a shuttle driver, saw my predicament and offered to bring me to the clinic for free. Not only did he take me there, but he gave me his number and told me to call when I was done so he could pick me up. Bubba went from shuttle driver to Trail Angel in an instant. I got in to see the doctor, got a prescription filled and received strict orders to take a week off the trail to recover. Bubba arrived to

Colt 45 and Carusoe

pick me up and brought me to the only motel in Bland. I tipped Bubba, rented a room and headed back out on the trail the next day. I had hiked 590 miles so far and had learned that a hiker who takes time off is sometimes never heard from again. Those that do come back, admit that it was hard. My cough would plague me for another month but it eventually faded away.

My second scare came during a long decent somewhere near the Shenandoah's. I was hiking along at a quicker than normal pace, feeling good, when I felt a sharp pain above my right knee. I knew something bad had happened, because of all the "pulls," "tweaks," "pops" and "creaks" I had experienced thus far, none was this painful. I took a short break, tried rubbing it, flexing it, stretching it and even pounding it (I know, but I was desperate!), but the pain wouldn't subside.

SAM "SAM I AM" DUCHARME

I was devastated! When I started this hike, I wasn't committed to finishing. I was happy being out on the trail doing something adventurous. Slowly, after the torture of the first month and hiking through the winter weather, I had built some commitment to finishing. Now failing because of an injury, was a result I wasn't prepared to accept.

I continued on, barely able to put weight on my right leg, and used my hiking poles the best I could to keep moving forward. I slowly limped the next six miles to a road crossing where I decided to go into town and buy a knee brace. I was down in the dumps because I felt like this injury was probably the end of my hike. I sat on my pack and took out my foam pad that I used for sitting on. Using a Sharpie, I wrote on my sleeping pad. I stood on an on-ramp holding this crude sign that said "Elkton" and forced a smile as the cars rolled off the road and onto the highway. There is a feeling you get when you are hoping for a ride and 30 cars drive by without picking you up. That feeling causes you to evaluate yourself. I evaluated myself and realized that my black shorts, black shirt, and black bandana on my head combined with my black hiking shoes and scruffy beard made me look more like a Hells Angel rather than a hiker. I was just about to jump into the bushes for a wardrobe change when a car stopped.

Thankfully, Enedina, a park ranger who works that stretch of Skyline Drive, knows a thing or two about hikers. My homeless-biker look didn't prevent her from stopping to pick me up. When this park ranger turned Trail Angel asked where I was heading, she hopped on the highway. She drove me to the nearest pharmacy where I bought a knee brace and a big bottle of ibuprofen. Seeing the difficulty I was having trying to walk, she insisted I stay off the trail for the rest of the day and offered to bring me to a campground to rest and spend the night. I conceded, and we were off to the nearest campground – but not before she drove me to a Burger King drive-thru for a Whopper... or two.

When we arrived at the campground, she asked me how I planned to return to the trail the next day. I explained that I would make a new sign and try to get a hitch. Enedina's willingness to help a stranger continued to bless me when she explained that she was going to church in the morning and would pick me up on the way. Afraid I might offend her, I explained that I didn't attend church regularly and I planned to return to the trail early due to my slowed pace with my knee and all. She laughed and told me she meant she would get me back to the trail before church... but if I changed my mind she would gladly bring me with her.

I managed to find my campsite. I hung my hammock between two huge RVs and experimented with my new knee brace. I felt like Steve Austin (the bionic man in the 70s TV series *The Six Million Dollar Man*) with all the Velcro, hinges and space-age materials wrapped around my leg! Even with all the bionics, I could see it wasn't going to be a cure. I took a few loops around the campground to test it out and settled into my hammock to enjoy my Whopper-high. The sounds of children fighting and parents yelling accompanied me while I dozed. I waited for the sun to set so I could pee under the cover of darkness, rather than limp all the way to the rest room. I didn't realize how spoiled I was – living on the trail.

Being accustomed to sleeping to the scurrying of forest animals and waking early to the sounds of singing birds for nearly two months, I wasn't prepared for a night of campground camping. *Men in Black* was playing by my feet and *The Lord of the Rings* by my head, but I guess I wouldn't have gotten much sleep anyway with the lights of the RVs glowing through the night like the Aurora Borealis. I couldn't help remembering my camping trips in northern Maine where the lights

Bean Counter

went out promptly when the Coleman fuel burned out. We slept soundly in our canvas tent and whenever we moved a puff of feathers would escape our army sleeping bags. These kids in the RV may never get to hear a loon over their Xbox. I actually felt bad for them.

In the morning, just about the time the campground got quiet, I packed up my camp, and sat at a nearby picnic table and put my new brace on. I couldn't help being amused hearing the dog barking at me from within one of the RVs as I limped away. When I got to the office parking lot, Enedina was waiting as promised, looking beautiful in her church dress. I threw my pack in the back and within 15 minutes I was back where she found me holding my sign. I was so grateful for her kindness I asked if she would take a picture with me so I would remember her whenever I looked through my photos. Of course she said yes, so I asked a woman who was parked at the trailhead preparing to go hiking, to take it for me. After the picture was taken, the woman said we looked so happy, and asked if Enedina was my wife? I replied that she wasn't my wife, but my Angel. No explanation was needed, and we both headed to our own churches. Another layer peeled away.

I was optimistic about using the new knee brace. I saw a lot of people using them and hoped it would be the answer to my problem. Immediately, however, I was disappointed. The knee pain hadn't let up and the ibuprofen wasn't touching it. Not only was the brace ineffective, it was causing terrible abrasions all the way around my knee. The skin was being rubbed off like a blister and gradually became more painful than the knee! I relented for the next 40 miles trying to tape my knee and using Neosporin on the sores which slowed my pace even more. I was panicking, feeling my journey was nearing its end, and I was angry. I wasn't angry at anyone or anything. I was angry because I was really enjoying the experience, the people and the trail. I really loved the excitement of discovering what was on the other side of the mountain, and around the bend and at the next town. Somewhere along the trail I went from not caring how far I got to only quitting if I sustained an injury. Now, having one, I was having a hard time accepting it. I was angry.

Now, obviously, you can hike when you are happy. You can hike when you are sad or lonely, too. When it comes to hiking when you are mad, you might as well just set up camp until your mood changes. When you hike mad, it just makes matters worse. You become less patient, your mistakes compound and you become mad at a variety of things that otherwise are immune to that human emotion. Also, when you are mad, the root fairies come out. I had just finished screaming at a red eft – the juvenile stage of a newt or salamander – when a root fairy snagged my foot causing me to fall flat on my face. The fall itself wasn't spectacular by any means. My knee being in such a painful state, however, threw me into a yelling fit normally only witnessed at a local Walmart. Shortly after, I found myself limping by a sign that said "Skyland Resort." After renaming it to the first ten, less-perky names in my head, I decided I needed a beer. It was late and I didn't much care if I set my hammock up in the dark, so I diverted from the trail.

Maybe it was the cheeseburger, maybe it was the two Miller Lites, but I felt better. I left in the rain and decided to hike five miles to a place called Byrds Nest Hut. I hiked most of the way with my head-lamp, slowly, nursing my knee. My mind was filled with thoughts of torn tendons and ripped cartilage, followed by surgical repairs and rehab. The thought of dropping out was almost as painful as my knee. The short break I took did little to keep my spirits up. I'm sure I shed a tear or two, but with all the rain and dark, no one would see it.

I arrived to the hut late, and although sleeping in the hut itself was never my intention, I was planning to camp at that location. It is almost always a good idea to plan to camp near one when you hike late into the night. Huts, shelters and lean-tos usually have good camping in the immediate area surrounding them, making set-up easier in the dark. This site was full, and I settled for a pair of trees surrounded by prickers. I got a little scratched up but at this point I didn't care. The rain was replaced with strong winds and my mood was gray as I set my hammock for the night. I had given my knee about 50 miles to improve and it looked like I had an injury that wouldn't let me finish. My anger turned to depression.

When daybreak came, I laid in my hammock listening to all the hikers milling around, cooking breakfast and chatting among them-selves. I didn't get up until they were all gone. This day was different for me. It didn't matter how many miles I hiked, what time I started or where I ended up. It would be my last day. I just waited for the last hiker to leave, carried all my gear into the hut and dropped everything in a wet pile on the sleeping platform. With my feet on the ground, I sat for a few minutes, then I laid back, not ready to pack up. What would I do? Return to Connecticut and return to work? Head up to

Maine and spend some time at my camp? Maybe go have my knee examined and listen to the doctor tell me the bad news? None of those options were appealing to me, so... I just laid there.

Eventually, I sat up. No sooner had I done that, Old Eagle Scout and Walnut hiked around the corner of the hut and exclaimed, "Sam I Am!" They were excited to see me because they wanted to introduce a third hiker they were hiking with: "RWB." Introductions were made and I was told that RWB was a medical professional and could examine my knee right there in the hut! When Old Eagle Scout and Walnut learned of RWB's profession, they told him about my knee and RWB offered to help track me down and take a look at it. They knew I wouldn't be far, so they set out to find me. Thankfully, they looked in that hut; they easily could have hiked past.

RWB conducted the examination right there on the low sleeping platform. He pulled and twisted, compared both knees, hummed a little, and checked out my abrasions. When he was done, he fished around in his pack, pulled out some 800mg ibuprofens and spoke: "I know that hurts like hell, but nothing is torn." I almost began to cry. He continued, "If you can take the pain, it won't end your hike." I was so happy I wanted to jump for joy! He went on to explain how I strained my tendon in my kneecap and I was wearing the wrong brace. He instructed me what to buy and advised me on wound care for the sores caused by the brace. He also explained that my knee would probably need a brace for the remainder of my hike, and rest would be prudent. Knowing I wouldn't rest, he handed me the ibuprofens and headed out. Here I was in the Shenandoah Mountains, ready to drop out of an epic journey, and out of the woods comes someone to tell me my time isn't up yet. *The trail will provide.*

This was a game changer for me. I would still deal with the pain. I now knew that I wasn't seriously injured and I wasn't causing damage.

I made some adjustments to my gait, bought the proper brace and made some gear adjustments. I removed everything from my pack that wasn't absolutely essential: extra clothes, Crocs, Kindle, iPod, cook stove, cup, toiletries, first aid supplies, spare batteries; everything except my sleeping system, food bag, water filtration system, pillow case and phone charger. I dropped 10 pounds and would eat a cold diet until my knee felt better.

11

Next Stop Harpers Ferry

The new knee brace and lighter pack felt better right away. I wasn't making reservations at the Katahdin Motel any time soon, but as "MoFo" would say, I was still "moving forward." The decision to remove nonessential items from my pack meant I was surviving on a cold diet. I really missed my stove! My evening meal of Knorr Rice Sides loaded with slices of summer sausage, along with a cup of hot mashed potatoes, was replaced by tortillas filled with tuna or salmon. In fact, all my meals were some sort of tortilla meal. During the day, I usually ate a couple tortillas with peanut butter, almond butter or Nutella with jelly. Some pepperoni or spam was usually thrown in for added protein. Yes, I'm serious. More tortillas were eaten in the morning with various combinations of those ingredients, along with a power bar. Some marketing genius declared the Snickers Bar as the "perfect food for hikers," so I ate a lot of those, too. As delicious as all that food was at the time, since returning from the trail, I have not eaten, nor do I plan to eat any one, or combination of, the food items mentioned here for a very long time.

Spring was in full foliage, shading me while I hiked Virginia's "flat and smooth" trails. The sun warmed the air and earth, stimulating everything into a growth explosion! The dull brown forests, and the dry grassy knolls that lay dormant as I passed a month ago, have woken and become full of colorful flowers and green leaves. Looking down into the valleys, hikers could see the farmland below as the dark soil was groomed into a patchwork of agriculture, promising a high yield of late summer crops. The sight inspired my imagination of dusty farmers with calloused hands and the thousands of people who rely on their hard work. If everything goes right, I'd be finishing my hike at about the same time those farmers were harvesting those same fields.

Naturally, due to its length, hikers spend a lot of time in Virginia. This, and the fact the newness of the trail has worn off, can sometimes lead to a condition referred by hikers as "The Virginia Blues." This is the loss of interest or motivation required to keep one foot moving in front of the other. Some hikers try to avoid this condition by paddling 100 miles parallel to the trail on the Shenandoah River (called aqua blazing); others take a break from the trail and realize they miss it within days; others call it quits and return home to their comfy beds and running water. Luckily for me, I was never plagued by this ailment. I found Virginia full of adventure.

Of all the trail states, I found Virginia the most diverse. There is plenty of elevation change, like the long climb up Apple Orchard Mountain where you climb over 3,000 feet only to descend as much on the other side. There are also open lands where you hike through rolling fields with free roaming ponies. Hiking beside Skyline Drive and crisscrossing The Blue Ridge Parkway was a welcome break from climbing mountains but that only lasted about 130 miles. Possibly my favorite section of the Appalachian Trail is in Virginia. Starting near Catawba, there is a thirty-mile stretch that brings you by a gigantic monolith called Dragon's Tooth, a popular ledge overhang called McAfee Knob, and a ledge-top hike across Tinker Cliffs. Just past all that, you hike under huge rocks that tower over the trail. How could anyone get the blues?

On a seemingly mellow day in southern Virginia, I had an experience that would thrill any hiker. I had been hiking alone for a few hours and silently crossed the 500 mile mark. This was a sweet moment for me. Aspiring thru-hikers will agree, mile markers and state lines are as sweet as a few honey buns purchased at a dirty convenience store, washed down with a Dr. Pepper. It was marked with the number 500 made with small stones in the center of the trail. I hiked past with my iPod playing "I wear my Sunglasses at night" for the 300th time and was enjoying the warm spring day. (I finally sent my iPod home to my friend Ray who loaded a new music playlist.) As I picked my way through the piles of pony poop in Grayson Highlands State Park, I detected some strange interference filtering through my earbud. Curious if I had finally worn out my playlist, I tugged on my earbud wire popping my earbud out of my left ear.

I'm deaf in my right ear, but I got in the habit of wearing the right earbud, too. Faster hikers thought I was ignoring them when they hiked up behind me, they could see my ear but I wouldn't answer. The same thing happened with two earbuds in, but the faster hiker could see the earbud wires coming out of both ears and politely tap my pole with theirs to get my attention. The earbuds kept the pesky bugs out of my ears, too.

My iPod wasn't malfunctioning, and it looked like I would have to listen to the same songs a while longer. I was turning in circles trying to locate the sound... to no avail (you have no directional hearing with only one good ear). The sound continued though, and before I could figure out what it was, a jet blasted into the sky right in front of me! I was on a flat mountaintop, and an F-15 was angling up from the valley below, crossing in front of me from my right to left! The jet was pulling a hard banking turn to the port side (pilot's left) exposing the top of the jet. It was so close I could see the pilot! The jet circled around the mountain I was standing on! To follow his flight, all I had to do is pivot in a circle, and then the pilot tossed the jet back to a level position. He or she must have pulled hard on the stick, because the jet climbed straight into the clouds! Okay, I know you think I am nuts, and for a second or two, I questioned myself. The noise from the jet was deafening and I could feel the roaring of the engine throughout my whole body! Before I could absorb what had just happened, another jet rose from the valley following the same route! My heart was pounding! I had been away from the news for a while, and briefly, I thought the worst was happening. I had been walking in the silent woods for about six weeks, and the excitement and overwhelming sound was thrilling! By the time my heart rate calmed down, "Maverick," "Goose," "IceMan" and "Hollywood" were probably 50 miles away. I didn't see that anywhere in my guide book. I remember thinking to myself, "No one is going to believe this."

Spring was bringing out all the beauty of the land and with the wakening of the forest, my spirits were high. Even the rain was warm! My knee was still slowing me down, but with the longer days I managed to stay with my bubble. There was a town ahead and I decided to go in and eat some real food, watch some TV and post a video at the local library. Several of the hikers in my bubble were stopping also, and we made plans to go out to eat together. I couldn't wait! Unfortunately, this would end up being one stop I would like to forget.

Motel Review

The town – Pearisburg, Virginia – was off the trail a bit; it was point-9 away. It looked like I'd be hitching. Some days the ole thumb just doesn't work, so after a half hour of standing on the hot asphalt, I hiked to the local motel. The horseshoe-shaped building was a survivor from the late '50s, when Howard Johnson's Motor Lodge was spreading its way across America. The building was painted to camouflage the HoJo's look, but with a little imagination, I could picture the vintage Town and Country station wagons parked in the angled slots inside the horseshoe. The old concrete pool inside the horse-shoe parking lot still held crystal clear water which looked inviting, even to a "germ-conscious" person. It was like stepping back into the past.

The long off-trail hike had me a little grumpy, but the anticipation of a cool shower and restaurant food was worth it. It was late afternoon when I checked in to the motel and to my surprise, they offered me a "hiker rate." I almost ran to my room when my key was handed to me; the last few days had been hot and I wanted nothing more than to stand in a cool shower. I entered the room like a SWAT team and made an abrupt stop as soon as I crossed the threshold. That is when I was hit by the stale cigarette stench that was trapped in the stuffy room. I stood in the doorway surveying the room like an investigator might observe a crime scene. The small space was slightly larger than a large closet with a twin-size bed against the left wall. Across from the ratty bed, there was an old desk with no chair. There was no TV or microwave and your only options for seating was on the bed, table or stained carpet. I slowly stepped backward closing the door before any more fresh air could drift inside to its death.

My lungs are not virgin to cigarette smoke. I grew up at a time where big colored glass ashtrays sat in the middle of the tables. The ashtrays were full of butts and ash and the adults filled the house with smoke. Back then people smoked inside, the cars came standard with ash trays, and second hand smoke wasn't even invented yet. Those were the days. Living in the 21st century, however, I have become accustomed to cleaner air and smoke-free rooms. I forgot to request a smoke-free room, so I headed back to the office for a room change.

The woman at the desk assured me that the room was a non-smoking room and if I wanted to change my room, it would cost me an additional 20 bucks. She also explained that the hiker rate only applied to those particular rooms because they were "economy" rooms, thus the rate increase for my new room. By then other hikers were waiting, so I flipped her another twenty, got a different key and headed to the "regular people" room.

I found my room door open and the cleaning staff inside. I was happy to see the non-smoking placard under the room number; maybe this really was a smoke free-room. It smelled marginally better, but due to the recent cleaning it smelled strongly of cleaning chemicals and Febreze. I could see it was a larger room with two beds. I was glad I was getting something for my 40% price bump! The motel staff finished up while I waited outside; it was only 10 minutes. Looking forward to our gathering for supper, I wasted no time jumping in the shower to cool off and change into my less-dirty clothes. I'm not usually a long shower taker, even when a few minutes longer might be advisable, but this shower would be shorter than most because the drain was clogged. Soon I was standing (complete with my trail runners on), in a filling tub! For most, that is no big deal, but for a germ conscious person like me, standing in a tub full of unknown DNA, strangers' hair and possible infectious diseases is disturbing! Finishing in the shower, I dried my trail runners and socks the best I could, and took a quick look around. I found the accommodations marginally better than the previous room, so I grabbed my money and headed out to join the other hikers for supper. I'd take a closer look when I got back.

By the time we left the motel, our group had grown to a dozen and we decided to go to a Mexican restaurant not far from the motel. What a time we had! Two months earlier, we were all adjusting to living out of a backpack in the woods. Now, as we all sat inside at a long table, eating with forks and wiping our lips with napkins, we felt like Mexican royalty. The food and drinks were consumed in an environment that resembled the closing scene of a Duck Dynasty episode, full of laughter and smiles. If it wasn't for the scruffy faces and hiking clothes, you would think we were lifelong friends. (Most of us would be; we just didn't know it yet). We all left with full bellies and new memories. My favorite memory of that meal was the look on Beerman's face when the server delivered eight plates of food after he ordered the special!

Full and happy, we all left that restaurant holding our bellies and groaning. It was blissful. On the way back to the motel, a few of us decided to go to the Goodwill store and see if we could find some replacement clothes. I'm sure we looked like a hoard of zombies slowly shuffling across the lighted parking lot with our stuffed bellies. By now, our clothes were pretty worn and stained and Goodwill was the perfect place to replace them. I had lost around 25 pounds and I needed a new shirt, the one I had was way too big and worn out. I had been hiking with swimming pool noodles, duct-taped inside my waist strap on my pack, due to the weight loss. I decided to look for a Virginia Tech shirt because we were in "Hokie" country, and I hoped it would help when I was hitchhiking. I found a bright orange one with a Grateful Dead skull and bought it for 50 cents.

Returning to my room, I decided to look around a bit. I shouldn't have. The Eau De Marlboro had strengthened with the door closed and the fluorescent light illuminated shades in the carpet I hadn't noticed before I left for supper. I propped the door and brought my backpack to Beerman's room so I wouldn't have to hike with cigarette smell on it for the next 100 miles. His room had been renovated in the last decade and the smell wasn't bad. While I aired-out the "deluxe" room, I took a moment to walk around and explore my digs. The first thing I did, like all hotel rooms, I tossed the bedspread on the floor. It was threadbare and pilly, and it had an unacceptable amount of little black hairs interwoven into the underside. Before continuing I felt the need to wash my hands. The sink was a beautiful light blue basin with stains and clear plastic knobs on each side of the plastic chrome faucet. The sink was plugged, too! Within seconds the basin was filling with dark stained water which left a ring as it slowly filtered through the unseen clog below. It was almost more than I could take. At this point I wanted to crawl into my sleeping bag liner, curl into the fetus position, and wait for sunrise. First, I had to use the bathroom.

A look into the tub showed a fine ring of trail dust marking the former water level. It was slightly higher than the water level left over from my earlier shower. I turned my attention to the toilet where I would deal with my next order of business. Toilets come in two distinct shapes: elongated and circular. Elongated toilets are more comfortable due to the amount of support the longer shape allows on the back of the legs. Circular toilets are generally used in smaller bathrooms where space is limited. The bathroom I rented for the night could have accommodated either just fine. The building maintenance department decided to use both; an elongated seat and circular bowl. By now you must think I am a Diva. I'm not. When you spend 20 years working in prisons where urine and feces are commonly used to assault officers, and blood and airborne pathogens are also a daily threat, you tend to watch what you touch... and breathe.

In this case, I touched the bowl. It is possibly the area with the highest concentration of nasty germs in any dwelling – residential or commercial. I was careful when I cleaned the seat, it needed it, but I didn't notice the mismatched seat/bowl combination until it was too late. The elongated seat positioned me to far forward on the circular bowl resulting in my most sensitive body part(s) resting on the cold porcelain. I was in GERM HELL! Thankfully, I still had plenty of baby wipes left! I waited until the next day where I could go to the bathroom in the woods – a clean peaceful environment.

In the meantime, I decided to walk around the town to escape my room from hell. It was late, the office was closed and I had already asked for an upgrade. I didn't have any hopes of finding a better room anyway. The only thing I had in the room were my toiletries and a sleeping-bag liner, so I left the door open to air out. I walked around the small town until 2 a.m., when I decided to return to the motel. All the businesses were closed, the roads were deserted and the one police officer in town kept repositioning himself to keep an eye on me. I'm sure I looked suspicious and I didn't want to waste his time, so I called it a night.

The room still stunk and I wasn't tired enough to lie on the bed, so I looked for a chair to sit on outside my door. I found a plastic deck chair near the dumpster. Ironically, it looked like the designated smoking area, and I took it back to my door and sat outside until morning. There wasn't the usual nightly activity, partly because the pool area was closed due to water quality issues, there was no ice maker and the parking lot was empty. I just dozed in my chair.

During the night, I plugged my phone in to charge it. When I searched for an outlet to use, I noticed the condition of the rest of the room. Stains that looked like a crime scene was prominent between the beds, the mattresses were also stained and threadbare, and the walls were filthy. I'm glad I didn't sleep inside.

The manager was adamant with the "no refunds" policy. It took three calls to the owner and my threats to call the Better Business Bureau before she refunded 20 dollars; after all, I had taken a shower and charged my phone. I was glad to leave; I had to get to the library to upload a video. This one would feature my first motel review.

Pearisburg Public Library has the slowest internet on the Appalachian Trail. It took all day to post my video and I couldn't wait to get back to the trail; Thanks to my disgusting motel room I had some unfinished business to attend to. Wearing my new shirt, I stuck my thumb out and promptly got a ride back to the trail.

The most notorious section in this state of lovers was called "The Rollercoaster." These 13 miles or so of trail is well known for its constant elevation changes. Although the climbs only lasted between 250 to 450 feet, they offered no rest between them. Sure, you could stop and rest, but there was no relief in the form of level ground. This section is the last hurrah for Virginia. With the West Virginia line close, it is like Virginia doesn't want to give up hikers without one last fight. I had the company of "Huckleberry Thug" through this section and as strenuous as the trail was, the heat and humidity would be our biggest challenge. The stifling air made it feel like I was hiking with a wet towel wrapped over my head. If you want to know what I'm talking about, just pull the blankets over your head while you read the next few pages.

Our enthusiasm was high when we stood near the sign noting the "extremely strenuous" section we were entering. We knew this sign was for section-hikers, after all we had come this far. How hard could it be? A few hours later, after escaping a violent thunderstorm by tucking under a stone ledge and nearly stepping on a copperhead that didn't detect my approach, I was getting the idea. The trail was exhausting. When we crossed the 1,000-mile mark, we took pictures. We looked like drowned rats! This monumental landmark was celebrated by lying in the soaked leaves for a brief rest. (I checked for copperheads first.)

Eventually, despite the heat, terrain and rain, we finished our day

1,000 miles

at a very unique hostel called Bear's Den. Just prior to getting there, we hiked by some scenic viewpoints. The area is a popular destination for day-hikers because of the view into the valley below. "Huck" and I were so spent; a quick glance to our left was the only attention it received from us. Tomorrow we would be out of this state and into Harpers Ferry, West Virginia.

Sadly, by the time I reach West Virginia, Carusoe, Colt 45 and Bean Counter leave the trail for good.

The unofficial halfway point

12

Halfway

I was excited as I walked across the bridge crossing the Shenandoah River because I had reached "The Unofficial Halfway Point" of the Appalachian Trail. The official halfway point was another 90 miles north in Pennsylvania, but at the moment, unofficial was close enough for me. The headquarters of the Appalachian Trail Conservancy (ATC) is located in Harpers Ferry, West Virginia, and it is a must stop for all hikers who are attempting a thru-hike. This was huge for me because it meant I had beaten the odds. Over half of the hikers have failed already. It also meant I was no longer counting miles hiked, but counting miles left – like turning and heading home. For me, it was a mental accomplishment as much as a physical one.

The ATC is a nonprofit organization dedicated to the conservation of the Appalachian Trail. Everything from painting blazes to land acquisitions is managed there. They also keep track of hiker data. Comparing the list of starters vs. the list of those who check in at the ATC, is helpful when compiling their statistics. Most aspiring thru-hikers take the short walk off-trail to have their photo and personal information permanently added to the current year's album, which is stored at the ATC forever. The headquarters offers hikers a room where hikers can rest, charge their phone, use the Wi-Fi or computers, or just hang out with the other hikers. When I got there... it was closed.

I arrived late in the day and took the short walk to the ATC, hoping it would be open. Finding it closed, I planned to spend the night somewhere and come back in the morning. My two best options were a hostel a few miles away or a religious community that welcomed hikers. The community seemed like a cultish option, so I chose the hostel. Fellow hikers who chose to stay at the religious community described the experience as "interestingly pleasant." I describe my hostel stay as "not totally unpleasant." I was just happy that I didn't have to do anything with tambourines.

The next morning on my way back to the trail, I stopped at the ATC where I had my picture taken, received my number, 586, and was officially added to the book. My spirits were soaring! The other hikers I met there were equally pumped and the atmosphere was like a subdued celebration; we were excited, but no one wanted to celebrate too soon. We still had a long way to go and too much respect for the trail to assume anything.

Red Hot, Stache, Rapunzel, Free Bird, MoFo, Forever, Hasselhoff, Old Eagle Scout, Walnut and Rocky Mountain High were also there documenting their passage and enjoying this new milestone. We'd made it halfway. We were in shape. We were all confident. That confidence paid off, too. Of the 10 people that were there when I showed up, all 11 of us finished.

I shot a video there to include in the latest episode and set out to find a place to upload it. There were a lot of people using the internet at the ATC, so I decided to look for another place. I hiked into the town hoping to find free Wi-Fi. What I found was a historic district. Being a historic district, there was a distinct lack of commercial businesses, like Starbucks or McDonald's (both of which are hikers' favorites). There were many shops and restaurants that catered to tourists, but while I walked around the area I didn't see any signs offering Wi-Fi use to customers. I decided to search for a strong signal using my phone and then ask the business owner if I could connect. Finding one belonging to a boutique, I entered the business and inquired. Veronica, the owner of the boutique, cautiously acquiesced.

For her act of kindness, Veronica got a stinky hiker hanging outside her boutique for the next few hours! I would've looked more at place under the steps than among her beautiful merchandise. I was happy she trusted me to use her network. I would go into her store a few times an hour to check the progress on my phone, which was hidden behind the Yankee Candles, then roam around outside. The internet was very slow, but I was happy to have it. While I was waiting outside under a small overhang, I was joined by some tourists who were trying to stay dry during a thunderstorm. They consisted of a Mom and Dad with their two boys, roughly 8 and 10.

The father, noticing my pack and "distinctive fashion," inquired about my hike. Upon learning I had been hiking for three months, the older son whispered something to his Dad. His Dad then asked me if I had seen Bigfoot. They were actually wearing Bigfoot T-shirts. I could tell by his serious look, he wasn't kidding; these people were serious about the mythic creature. I told them a true story:

"I was all alone, camped in a narrow gap between two steep mountains, deep in the forest. It got dark earlier than normal because of the dense cover of leaves above and the narrow gap. I had to go a little further off the trail because the brush was so thick, but I finally found

a place to camp. I set up my hammock and tarp, ate supper and went to sleep. Somewhere in the night, I was woken by a heavy tug on my tarp. Something had bumped into one of my tarp lines, so it was close! I let out a loud yell and whatever it was ran off. It was so dark I couldn't see what it was, but I laid there wide awake listening to the forest. A few minutes later I heard footsteps coming back! They came closer and closer until they stopped close to my hammock; all I could hear was sniffing! I let out another yell and it ran off again. I never saw what it was then either, but whatever it was, it didn't act like a deer or bear! Was it Bigfoot? Your guess is as good as mine."

They looked at each other like I had just proved, after all, that there must be a Bigfoot. The father shook my hand with both of his and thanked me. The two boys, who were previously shy, also shook my hand. When Mom shook my hand, she gave me the same serious look. She seemed to be thankful that I took them seriously, I was just glad I had a story to tell them.

Returning to the boutique and over the course of the afternoon, I engaged Veronica in light conversation and despite my contrast to her beautiful store and merchandise, she was so nice and welcoming. It was late afternoon when my video finished. I thanked her again and we said our goodbyes. When I walked over the bridge above the Potomac River, I looked back on that old village – with the brick and wooden buildings crowded together on the hillside – and thought, "I would like to come back here someday." Another layer was left in Harpers Ferry.

Much later, in late July, I heard that Harpers Ferry sustained a huge fire in the historic district. I contacted Veronica and was saddened to hear that her boutique burned out. She lost everything. It was a somber reminder that while my world consisted of a small strip of dirt, it was still connected to the "real world." This realization reminded me to appreciate my now, because things happen fast... even at 2.5 mph.

The original Washington Monument in Maryland

13

Four State Challenge

 West Virginia has about four miles of trail before it leads into Maryland. From there it's about 40 miles to Pennsylvania. Some of the hikers who haven't felt enough pain yet, like to do the "Four State Challenge." This requires the hiker to start in Virginia, hike through West Virginia and Maryland, and cross into Pennsylvania. The challenge is to do it in less than 24 hours. I did notice a few proud hikers sharing their feat with fellow hikers, but I tried to be a little more modest; I accomplished the 24-hour marathon in just under 72 hours.

Despite the short distance between Virginia and Pennsylvania, West Virginia and Maryland have a lot going on. The walk leaving Harpers Ferry follows a long tow road with a swampy canal on your West side and the wide Shenandoah River on the East. The beauty lays in its flatness. Find a public restroom before you leave Harpers Ferry though, as Rocky Mountain High can attest, there isn't much room on either side to use the little girl's tree.

By the time I got to Pen Mar Park on the Maryland/Pennsylvania line, I had been treated to some of Maryland's hidden treasures. Due to its rich history, I had the privilege of visiting a couple of state parks. When I hiked into Gathland State Park, it was late in the day and I stopped to fill up on water. State parks are a welcome sight for hikers because they often offer clean water, bathrooms, garbage cans to get rid of our trash (Leave No Trace) and my favorite... benches!

I saw another hiker sitting on a bench, so I decided to visit with him. As I approached I could see he was distressed. Before I sat down I could see he looked around my age, maybe a little younger, and he was spent. His clothes were soaked through, his gear was carelessly scattered around his feet and his hair was matted to his head with sweat. I was pretty soaked myself, the humidity was high and we had a few summer-like thunderstorms pass through; I understood his misery.

I introduced myself and as I sat, I noticed hard-boiled eggs, some smashed, some still whole, and I asked if he dropped them? "Nope, threw them there, let the birds eat 'em!" I thought that strange because to me, it seemed like it would be a sick form of cannibalism, besides they were more likely to draw the attention of a raccoon or skunk first. Licking my chops, I asked him if he minded if I picked up a few for myself. He let me. I love eggs – they are the perfect food; they remain untouched by human hands until consumed. While I was picking through them, looking for survivors, he admitted throwing them out in a fit of frustration. That also accounted for the gear on the ground. He was getting ready to throw it all in the garbage can holding the restroom door open.

He was on his first overnight hike with his three friends. His knee hurt, had blisters on his feet and he hadn't seen his friends in two days. (He was learning the joys of hiking.) Due to the fact he "was never hiking again," he was throwing all his gear away. I tried to encourage him to rethink his decision and that he just bit off a little more than he could chew. "Nope, I'm done hiking." I stuck around for a while, eyeballing the pile of gear as he took handfuls to the garbage can. He was camping close to the park and his Mom was picking him up back here in the morning. He looked mad at each piece of gear he threw out, and he was especially rough with his "bad" pack.

In true aspiring thru-hiker form, I unashamedly saved all the packaged food he was throwing out. After all, I was a real "long-distance backpacker" now, having hiked through 5 of the 14 states along the AT; I could handle the extra weight. I regretted not having my stove; he threw out some good dehydrated meals. I saved the oatmeal crèmes, remainder of the eggs, Cliff Bars and about two pounds of trail mix from the raccoons. *The trail will provide.* I felt like I was looking at a version of myself three months earlier. I left him to his bench where he could rest his knee and give his blisters a break, and I went to read the information plaques around the park. Before I left him, I asked if he had a trail name. "No, just Dave." I told him he should call himself "Bill" or "Katz," after two famous people with ties to the trail, and because they, too, had tossed some gear on their hike.

The information on the plaques was very interesting. I was standing on the spot where the Battle of South Mountain took place, the first major battle of the Civil War fought in Maryland. I followed the plaques around, each leading to the next, like chapters in a book. It took little imagination to picture the soldiers in their uniforms, armed with heavy muskets taking cover along the stonewall facing the gap in the mountains. I noticed a few hikers pass, crossing the grassy area past the remnants of a stone structure, but I sacrificed the last hour of light to read each plaque. At one point, the park ranger came over to me to tell me the bathrooms were going to be locked up for the night. I thanked him and told him if he was looking for hiking gear,

Looking west on Annapolis Rocks in Maryland

there were a couple Nalgene bottles, a water filtration system and rain jacket in the garbage, along with miscellaneous other pieces of hiking gear he might want to pick through.

I headed out, crossing the wet grassy field, past the remains of a great stone structure, and into the woods. Near dark, I picked a pretty woodland spot just short of a shelter, and set up for the night. About 20 yards away, on the trail, I saw "Just Dave" trudging by. I told him there was plenty of room to set a tent and invited him to join me. I was surprised at his efficiency at setting his tent, and within twenty minutes I heard him snoring away. When I woke in the morning, he was packed up and gone. That was the last I heard of "Just Dave."

Later that day, I met up with "EZ Stryder." We hit it off as soon as we met, due to our shared language intricacies. Most of my crude language, cultivated from the prisons, was slowly changing to a more publicly accepted form of communication, but my Northeast roots would expose me to like-speaking hikers. Normally, I wouldn't be too sure of a man hiking in a dress, but his great personality shined through immediately. He called it a kilt, I told him that's what the inmates said when they talked about the murder they committed. I don't think he liked it when I called it what it was... a dress. Being from Massachusetts, not 40 miles from my home, EZ and I had a lot in common. He is also an avid outdoorsman, and we rolled right into fishing and hunting stories. We hiked and talked, mostly about trout fishing and turkey hunting, both of which, we sacrificed this spring to hike.

We ate lunch in a park pavilion along the trail, sharing our break with a family who peppered us with questions for their children's sake. Questions were common when we ran into "muggles." If you're a Harry Potter fan, you know muggles are "people who lack any magical abilities." On the trail, this term has been borrowed to describe non-hikers. By the time we were done dazzling the kids with adventurous stories of big bears and rattlesnakes, it will be a miracle if they ever step foot out of the house again! Having filled their duties entertaining the kids for an hour, the parents tossed EZ and I a couple snacks, herded the kids back to the air conditioning and DVDs, then drove away in their Mercedes SUV. It was a fun break, but I forgot my brand new New England Patriots hat hanging on a nail when we left!

Shortly after our break, and filling up with water at a hand pump, we arrived at the original Washington Monument. Steeped in history, this forty-foot stone tower was built on the ridge of the mountain, offering views of the valleys on both sides. The short climb inside the tower led to an observation floor surrounded by a sturdy wall of stone. The warm breeze was a welcome relief to the heat and humidity of the forest below. The scenery has changed since it was built, but I'm sure the feeling of awe I got looking out was just as powerful then, 188 years ago. I can't understand why the Four State Challenge is a thing... There is so much to see.

Neither EZ nor I paid much attention to our trail guide, so we were curious when we saw a small sign that said "Annapolis Rock." Neither of us spoke, we just looked at each other, shrugged our shoulders and headed that way. At this pace it's a miracle I ever made it out of Maryland.

We hiked through a sparsely inhabited primitive campground, stopping a couple times to shrug our shoulders at each other again, but continued on. We were rewarded when we arrived on a huge rock cliff. The sun had dried the ledges from the earlier thunderstorms and the steamy mist that often follows was drifting above the trees 1700 feet below. The breeze bordered on windy, drying our shirts on the hot rocks. I was experimenting with this clothes-drying technique after hearing it from another hiker. He recommended a hot paved road, but this area was safer, if you don't get too close to the edge.

We decided to camp here and the caretaker let us use a site in a more remote part of the area. (He probably saw EZ's dress and thought we were on our honeymoon.) It turned out to be an awesome campsite, and despite our plans to go check out the stars at the cliffs after dark, we both slept through the night and shrugged our shoulders at each other in the morning.

By the time EZ and I made it to Pen Mar Park, the scuttlebutt on the trail was that Scott Jurek, an ultramarathoner, was going to pass us. Jurek was attempting to break the record for the fastest assisted thru-hike. Basically, he would walk/run about 50 miles a day, assisted by his support crew who met him along the way with food and supplies. At night, his team would meet him and he slept in a van. Most of the hikers I met didn't give him much thought, not really considering him a hiker at all. The sheer fact that he was covering that distance over the same rugged terrain we were hiking, however, was winning us over.

EZ Stryder

Pen Mar Park has a beautiful multi-level overlook pavilion, only a few feet from the trail where EZ and I waited to see Jurek pass. The word was out and supporters, on and off the trail, congregated, while we enjoyed the view of the region from an elevation of about 1,400 feet. We waited for almost three hours before giving up on him. It was getting close to dark, so we all set out.

We were starting to doubt the rumors that we might see the record attempter, so we moved on with a plan to camp near the trail, just in case. Just beyond the park the trail takes a sharp left turn on a gravel area and crosses a railroad track. The nearest white blaze is across the track and with daylight fading, it was hard to see where the trail went.

After crossing the track and with light fading fast, I decided to return to the graveled surface and scratch an arrow into the ground on the chance Jurek passed during the night. Scratching in the dirt was common at tricky turns, because so many people miss these turns. The wrong way becomes as worn as the trail.

As I was dragging my heel and finishing with my eight foot arrow, EZ, Piper, Old Eagle Scout and Forever, all started yelling to me: "TRAIN!" The tracks were less than 20 yards away, but the panic in their combined voices triggered me to run towards them as if they were warning me a great big bear was about to maul me! I felt like I was in the train scene from Stand by Me. All at once, I saw their happy faces freeze in terror; I wasn't going to make it I was actually going to get hit by the train! I skidded to a stop as the train barreled past. It came around a bend from my right side and before I could see it, it was here. The engineer looked terrified. Of all the ways to die on the trail, I almost bit it by a train. How close was it? My feet stopped at the wooden ties.

This shook us all up a bit. They thought they had called me to my death, and I felt stupid for almost getting hit by a train. We stopped for a minute a few yards away from the track, at the Mason-Dixon Line, to shake it off. We had stepped into Pennsylvania and into the North! This landmark quickly chased our latest drama away, and we took turns taking pictures next to the sign. We even enlisted the help of a section-hiker to take a group picture for us – six times. We still had hopes of seeing Jurek as he passed so we headed into the woods where we were happy to find a spot that would accommodate all of us. I stuck to my norm and set up a little deeper in the woods. By now it was headlight dark and as I sat on my ground tarp having my baby-wipe bath, I saw a line of headlamps coming down the trail.

I could hear the excitement as my group was cheering him on as he passed, shouting "Good Luck!" I watched from under my tarp, buck naked with a baby wipe stuck in my toes, while Jurek jogged past with his supporters following him in a long line of bobbing headlamps. It reminded me of a scene from Forrest Gump. EZ ran with him for a while, and forty minutes later he returned looking like a dog who gave up on a deer. We gathered around him as he recounted his experience. According to EZ, Jurek is a very nice guy who held a conversation with him while they jogged. Jurek even stopped for a photo before he picked up his pace and EZ headed back. Scott Jurek eventually broke the record, and every story of hiker encounters I heard, they were all about the same; very friendly, easy to talk to and stopped for pictures. Yes, he won us over.

The next few days were lackluster, compared to the previous few. West Virginia and Maryland were great. I hiked and camped with fun people, saw some interesting historical sites, had a near death experience and crossed the Mason-Dixon Line. Now, EZ, Forever and Old Eagle Scout went off the trail for massages. I was hiking alone and I still hadn't crossed the official halfway point! I had quietly celebrated in Harpers Ferry, had my halfway point recorded with the ATC and had mentally crossed halfway. So for nearly a week, it was like I was rehiking the 90 miles leading up to the halfway point. When I reached "the official halfway point" near Pine Grove Furnace Park, it was marked with a sign, and I had none of the excitement I felt when I stopped at the ATC. I took a picture and was glad it was official. Then, about point-2 later, I passed another sign with American flags posting the halfway point. By then I didn't care.

Red Hot

14

Southern Pennsylvania is Beautiful

 It was an odd feeling when I finally passed the official halfway point(s) in Pennsylvania. I was hiking alone and I had some time to reflect. I felt a great sense of accomplishment; the experience was much harder than I expected. Getting to this point was due to the camaraderie of my fellow hikers and the outpouring of support from viewers. Without them I might have given up. I had been on the trail for a long time and despite my improved conditioning, increased daily mileage and growing trail family, it was depressing at the same time... all that way, and all that time, yet I was only halfway.

Pennsylvania is about 229 miles long. The actual mileage changes from year to year because of natural or man-made reasons, but one thing is for sure, the mileage in Pennsylvania is memorable. If you look at the elevation profile of this state, you would look forward to an easy stroll from Maryland to New Jersey. When your soles hit the ground, however, this state proves to be about as challenging as any on the trail.

Okay, follow me here: The Blue Ridge Mountains are actually part of the Appalachian Mountains Range. It starts in southern Georgia and stretches into Pennsylvania. I promised not to get to heavy on the geography, and so I won't. All you have to know is the Blue Ridge Mountains end in southern Pennsylvania and you have to cross the Great Appalachian Valley to the Larger Appalachian Mountains Range, to the west. When you reach those mountains, turn north and keep hiking.

The Great Appalachian Valley is a huge valley starting in Quebec and it goes all the way down to Alabama, or about 1,200 miles. It is more commonly recognized by the regional names like Shenandoah Valley, Lehigh Valley, Hudson Valley, etc. At this point, the trail crosses the valley over to the Larger Appalachian Mountains Range via the Cumberland Valley. The nice thing about that is that there is a break in all the mountain climbing for a day or so.

The valley requires a day worth of hiking through flat agricultural lands. The nutrient-rich soil that I walked on once blanketed the rocky ridges of the ranges I traversed. The trail leads through miles of fields, full of corn, wheat and grass. The open fields were a stark change to the shaded mountains and ridgelines, and the soft soil was a moderate trade for the cover of trees. The day I crossed it was very hot and humid and the mountains I was hiking towards would occasionally become lost in the haze. Thunder rolled from the low clouds that carry the summer storms and they threatened to burst any moment. I could actually see the gray rainfall from some of them. When I looked back, the sky was blue with white fluffy clouds; I was walking directly into it.

During the day, I began hiking with "Teach." He was a tall hand-some guy who looked like a Subaru model. We hadn't met before, so he described his three-year plan to complete the whole trail. He was carrying out a big wet sleeping bag that someone left in the woods as we passed through the fields. This was the second leg of his hike. Last year he hiked the southern half and the northern half would be done in two sections. He spoke with loving enthusiasm as he described the students in his class, hence the name "Teach." I followed, lost in the wake of Bounce Fabric Softeners and Irish Spring soap, while we tried to reach the mountains on the far side of the valley.

We managed to get through the valley just as the big storm hit. We agreed to split a room at a resort in Boiling Springs where we could escape the storm and eat at a buffet. The thunder had been rocking the valley for a couple hours, but just as we approached the big awning in front of the resort, all hell broke loose. The rain began pouring down and the wind gusted, bending trees and tearing the leaves from the branches. Red Hot and Free Bird joined us as we stood inside the glass doors watching the torn leaves flow past in a torrent. Happy and Walnut had just checked in as well, and we all agreed to meet up after some well-needed showers.

We were seated in a large dining room filled with guests who were eating at the upscale buffet before attending a play held somewhere on the premises. Dressed in our finest hiking clothes, we stuck out like a sore thumb. The food was amazing and we enjoyed walking through all the muggles as we repeated our trips between our big round table and the buffet. The rain outside was drowning out the voices in the dining room and thunder shook the building every few seconds. I was waiting for the power to go out but it never did. We would've been quite a sight, six-headlamps shining on our plates in the dark.

There are a few events on my journey that rise to the top-moments that define the entire trip. This is one of those events. It wasn't obvious at the time, we were just six men who were sharing a meal, but the further I walked from that table in Pennsylvania, the more I appreciated it. The trail would shuffle us up, crossing our paths from here to Maine, but it was a chance to sit down for a couple hours and forget the trail. We were a bunch of dads missing our kids and sharing stories from home.

Freebird, Sam I Am, Teach, Happy and Walnut.
(Photo by Red Hot)

We sat long after the play crowd left the dining room and the buffet was disassembled. The staff cleaned the large room, wheeled the dirty plates and glasses from all the other tables while we sat under the lone row of dimmed lights. We finally tossed our napkins on the table and left after Red Hot finished telling us all a poignant story from his youth. There wasn't a dry eye among us, and I'm touched that he shared it. He was much more than his humble appearance let on, and I looked forward to crossing paths with him again before we finished our hike.

We lost track of each other after the meal, each going our separate ways, with our own plans: Free Bird went home to take care of some family issues; Happy went to New York City to meet his wife; and Teach and I just headed back to the trail. I wouldn't see Red Hot again until Connecticut.

The trail was littered with debris from the violent storm and hikers who took refuge in the shelters gave us stories of falling trees and intense lightning strikes, but thankfully, there were no stories of injuries.

I continued hiking with Teach, arriving in Duncannon, Pennsylvania, by midafternoon. We stood on a rock looking down into the town which sits on the shore of the Susquehanna River, and we were excited to drop down in for a visit. The rocky decent off the mountain, and the sweltering heat called for a beer, so we decided to stop at the Doyle Hotel.

"The Doyle" as it is called, is a hotel that has been around longer than the trail itself. Teach and I would meet up there later, I had been out of the south for a few days and wanted to see if I could find some sweet tea. I found some at a little store on the edge of town and bought a gallon. It was much hotter in the valley, so I sat in the shade of a maple tree with Tunz and Flapjack, who were planning to go to the Doyle also... but after a short siesta.

Duncannon has a rich past being next to river and all, but when I walked up the main street towards The Doyle, it was clear that time had changed things. The old wooden buildings that lined the street had been covered with vinyl siding, some in disrepair, with cloudy windows where shoppers used to view new merchandise. Others that were

SOLE SEARCHING ON THE APPALACHIAN TRAIL

still inhabited were worn and crooked, despite the modern facelift. One brick building had a huge mural painted in beautiful colors, the gem of the street.

As I got closer to this landmark, the businesses along the road looked similar to those on the edge of town, only better maintained. Some of these had porches for the upstairs tenants, with a view of the street below. No one was sitting out there when I went by; they were probably sitting inside in the air conditioning. There were plenty of cars parked on both sides of the road, nosed in at an angle, but other than a few trucks driving past, the street was dead. I walked right up the middle.

You can't miss the old motel. It is a huge brick building with four floors, a full porch on the second floor and a distinctive stone arch outside its corner entrance. The porch covers the sidewalk, giving the building its impressive footprint. The arched window frames show traces of fine masonry, but the graceful arches held windows from a different time – not original, but not modern, somewhere in the middle.

I went in to find Pat and Vikki, the proprietors, hard at work serving cold beer and food to a barroom full of hikers. Most of them were familiar but it was especially nice to see Coz there, too. I hadn't seen him since the Smokies. The barroom (baah-roohm, as we say in New England) had the feel of a local VFW where you knew everyone, and I was greeted with a raucous welcome when I entered. I joined them for lunch and a couple Yuenglings, Pennsylvania's most famous beer.

Before long, the clock on the wall pointed well past hiker midnight, and Teach, Coz and I decided to head out. You can rent a room at The Doyle, but we opted for a campground on the far edge of town. Before we left town, however, we decided to stop in at a pizza parlor (pronounced "paah-lah") and join some more hikers who were having a few Yuenglings of their own. The waitress led us out back where we were seated on a modern patio/deck overlooking the train tracks, and where we were seated with fellow hikers. Compared to The Doyle, It was like fast forwarding a half century!

The next couple hours were spent with an interesting trio: "Cap" (Georgia), "Goose" (Georgia) and "Spice" (Minnesota). They called

The Doyle

themselves the "Packing It Out" crew. During their hike, they were picking up every piece of trash they found. Cigarette butts, candy wrappers, plastic bags, empty tuna packages – everything. By the time I met them, they had already picked up over six hundred pounds of trash! I proudly told them about Teach and how he lugged a wet, dirty sleeping bag out of the woods. They instantly bonded. When they asked me what I picked up, I reminded them that I had been following them and they hadn't left anything. I don't think they bought it. By the time they finished, they picked over half a ton of trash off the AT!

After finishing our second full meal in four hours, Teach, Coz and I backtracked to the white blazes, followed them through the residential section of town and back to the railroad tracks. The campground office, a construction trailer, was closed for the night so we self-camped in the dark. There were absolutely no lights within the campground so we searched for our own spots to camp, following our headlamp beams through the empty campground.

I camped on the shore of the Susquehanna River. The slow flowing river seemed peaceful as its smooth surface reflected the lights from the highway traffic on the bridge above. The rhythmic sound of rubber tires colliding with uneven expansion joints echoed across the water like duck hunters on opening day. The campground was long and narrow, sandwiched between the river and the railroad tracks. Every half hour or so, the sounds of the highway would fade when slow freight trains ground passed 50 yards away. The whole setting was a sensory overload! I could feel the vibrations from the freight cars travel from the roots of the trees, right up the tree and through my hammock!

For a small quiet town in Pennsylvania, Duncannon is a busy place. When we walked across the bridge looking down into the Susquehanna, we laughed together at the peaceful chaos we experienced in that town.

The 501 Shelter is a unique shelter and it marks the end of the mild trail through southern Pennsylvania. It also marks the beginning of roughest stretch I would personally endure during my hike. The

Lehigh Gap in Pennsylvania

shelter itself wasn't built for the purpose of housing hikers; it was previously a pottery shop or something. The fact that it had two doors, running water, four walls, and picnic tables inside, made it a virtual mansion. The close proximity to Rte. 501 and a close pizza parlor made it a must stop for a hungry hiker like me.

I arrived during a long stretch of rain that would last several days, so pizza and a roof appealed to me. There were eight or nine hikers there when I arrived and the rumor of pizza was confirmed by the pile of empty pizza boxes left by the previous hikers. The rain on the domed skylight was a constant reminder of our good fortune, and good cell reception allowed us to call the number on a menu. Life is good.

By the time the pizza arrived, the shelter was filling up. When Mowgli and Big Easy arrived, I let Mowgli have my bunk and hung my hammock across the room. As you know, I normally avoid sleeping in shelters, but the shelter had 12 individual bunks around the room and plenty of room for everyone to move around. The hikers were all well known to me, and there was a fun pizza-party atmosphere among us. It was one of those nights where everything was perfect.

The following day I was sick. I left early; after all, my hammock was hanging in the middle of the room and I didn't want to be a nuisance. When I heard the first air mattress deflating, I packed up and headed out. The trail was one long puddle with lush vegetation on both sides. There wasn't any sense trying to avoid the water, the ground was saturated through the woods, too. The only way through was to walk straight down the trail.

I don't know if the pizza was too much of a shock to my system, or I picked something up from the shelter, but I had to go use the little boy's tree, FAST! By mid-Pennsylvania using the woods when I had to go was a normal. Using this method in the rain, however, never gets easier. Remember the story about the sock decomposing in a hole? Here is the rest of the story:

Within 10 minutes of leaving the shelter I was racked with sharp cramps. I hoped to delay my off-trail visit until the rain let up, so I continued sloshing through the water and black mud. When the second wave of cramps hit, I realized the severity of my situation; it was critical. I dropped my pack in the three inches of flooded trail and plowed through the prickers. In all the excitement and last second deployment, I left my post-poop supplies in my pack. I was stuck in the Technique #2 position 10 yards from the trail with 10 people heading my way at any moment! I unlaced my right hiking shoe, removed my sock and sacrificed it in the name of decency.

When I arrived back at my pack, there was no time to hang around and dig out a clean sock, the cramps were back with a vengeance and I only had enough time to grab a Ziploc of baby wipes and run back; I looked like a kid trying to run in the ocean, lifting my knees and feet as high as I could to avoid the sharp thorns. Every time I finished cleaning up, another wave of contractions would hit. I wasn't going anywhere.

I managed to hike a mile or so, but I was spending more time off the trail than on the trail and I was overcome with weakness. After I buried a pair of underwear and began shaking, I decided to set my hammock and try to warm up. I took off my clothes and tried to dry off the best I could, but I continued with my urgent dashes to the bushes every 10 minutes or so. I stopped putting my shorts on after the third or fourth trip. I eventually fell asleep allowing me some relief for a couple hours.

If there was a time when I'd rather have been in a dry bed with soft linens, this was it. Being sick, outside in the wet woods was mentally defeating. My mind was trying to figure out what was going on. Was it bad pizza? Giardia? Flu? Dehydration? I didn't know, so I avoided hikers and kept hiking.

My progress was slow I had no appetite, and was losing even more weight; I needed to get back on track. I decided to go into town for supplies. I was shocked to learn I had lost 52 pounds, and I needed to gain some back to regain my energy. My cold diet wasn't working.

I began to take a different approach. I bought protein powder to regain weight and started spending more time off-trail searching out diners, restaurants and bars for hot meals. I would hitch to the first place I came to (the locals were very helpful), and hitch back after a big meal. One of my favorite stops came when a nice couple picked me up and brought me into town a few miles from the trail. I spotted a sign near the road that advertised "Pulled Pork." When I told the people who picked me up that this was fine, they quickly said, "That is a rough place." I didn't care, I would risk it for pulled pork. Besides, the farther from the trail I went, the harder it was to get back.

SOLE SEARCHING ON THE APPALACHIAN TRAIL

Reluctantly, they pulled in and popped the hatch so I could get my pack. The light green Subaru looked cute parked among all the Harley Davidson motorcycles and jacked-up pickups. I heard the door locks click as I waived, and they sped off.

They were right – it looked like a tough place. I dropped my pack at the door and went in. It took a minute for my eyes to adjust to the dark room while I found a stool at the bar. All eyes were on me as I walked around the horseshoe bar. I lifted my chin slightly when someone would lock eyes with me; it means "what's up" in "tough guy." When I found a stool, I slowly turned to the bartender and in my toughest voice ordered, "Cold iced tea and pulled pork, please."

Come to find out, these people were as interested in the trail as everyone else. Before long I had a group of bikers wearing their club vests, surrounding me as I answered questions and showed pics from my phone. When I showed them a picture of my Harley, they offered to pay for my meal and give me a ride back to the trail. I accepted as long as I didn't have to ride on the back of a bike. When I left, almost everyone saw me off with handshakes and backslaps. Then a skinny guy with a black vest and a red bandana drove me to the trail in his truck. Another layer... gone.

These side trips for meat along with the protein (I made shakes), slowly began to build me back up. I made a large shake (32 oz.) in the morning and another at lunch. It was a ridiculous amount of calories but like every other aspect of hiking, I had no idea about nutrition either. I added drink mixes into the shakes for variety, and at lunch I imagined it was steak or pork. I felt better, and within a couple weeks I gained nine pounds. I would gain another five or six by the time I finished in Maine.

While I was dealing with low energy, weight loss, slowed progress and off trail foraging, the trail changed dramatically. I expected the rocks that northern Pennsylvania was famous for, but there is no over stating their ability to wear down a hiker's mind and body. The last 100 miles or so before New Jersey is like walking on a stone wall. There are big rocks, knife-edged slabs, giant boulders that require you to put your poles away so you can use your hands, and little toe-grabbers that don't move when you stub them. I only knew one person who wasn't fazed by the relentless rocks in Pennsylvania; it was "Happy." Nothing could affect his perpetual, well... Happiness.

All these rocks require your constant attention. Looking for white blazes can actually be hazardous! I was glad to be a hammock sleeper in Pennsylvania, because there were places where it was impossible to sleep on the ground without a rock under you. When I crossed into New Jersey over the Delaware River, I actually cried; Pennsylvania beat me down.

Trail Closed!

15
Wildlife

 By the midpoint of my hike, I had already had my share of wildlife encounters. When you think of six months in the woods, people tend to think of the bears flipping logs for grubs and deer grazing for acorns. I can tell you, there is a lot more going on out there. For instance, the morning EZ and I woke up when we camped at Annapolis Rock, I reached down from my hammock to get my glasses, which I kept in my shoe at night, and came face to face with the biggest, hairiest spider I ever saw! When EZ looked out of his tent, I was chasing it into the brush with a stick!

Bears

When it comes to bears, I wasn't worried. I have spent years in the woods and usually, if you get close to these animals, they run off before you even know they're there. I was wrong again. My experience with bears is limited to hunting in Maine and Canada. The bears up there avoid human contact. On the trail, the bears are acclimated to sharing the forest with hikers; in fact, they depend on them. A careless hiker who leaves their food bag available is exactly what a bear looks for. It took me a while to understand why the bears just stood and watched, or slowly walked away, instead of crashing through the woods to hide. We weren't a threat to them, and often times, they found easy food around us. So essentially, we represented food to them. No, I don't mean they want to eat us, but leftovers on a creek bank left from washing out a pot of rice or a food bag full of goodies. It had to be better than ants.

My first close encounter was in the Smokies. I was camped in one of the few authorized campsites, which was deep in a giant bowl surrounded by huge, bare hardwoods. I casually took a picture of a sign noting "dangerous bear activity in the area" before hiking down to the site. I was with Dusty Pilgrim, Carusoe and Colt 45. I was camped away from them, as usual, about 75 yards up on the side hill. At the time, I was facing away from them, kneeling on the ground, fishing through my pack. From the fire pit, I heard Dusty half whispering, half yelling to me to "Get your camera!" I knew from his tone, something was going on, we had been together long enough that he knew I wanted to catch everything on video for YouTube.

I stood and looked back at the guys, and they were all pointing back at me. Actually, they were pointing behind me; I still had no idea what was going on. Dusty, in his cool Clint Eastwood voice, said, "Bear." I looked back and sure enough, there was a bear on the other side of my hammock! I didn't see him at first because my tarp was up, and it blocked my view up the hill. I stepped up on a large stone and videoed him as he slowly walked by the campsite, stopping every 20 yards or so to check us out. He would stop, slowly turn his head and stare for about ten seconds, before he silently moved again. He was a mature bear, the biggest I've ever seen, and it was eerie. I say he, because it was late spring and there were no cubs tagging along. Of course, it is just a guess. I got a couple minutes of video, and in my excitement I forgot I was standing on a large rock. I fell down the hill and slammed my face into the ground. When that loud high-pitch ringing stopped, I was thrilled to have that footage for next week's episode.

I had several bear encounters, some like the one I just mentioned were only a few minutes. Others were a brief glimpse or a surprise meeting. These moments generally shocked both of us, sending the bear into the bushes and me standing there wondering, "Did that just happen?" or "Am I hallucinating?" On one occasion, I was the one who had to back off.

I was jamming to some rowdy tunes, be-bopping along, when the trail swung to the west around a large oak tree. When the trail gets close to these huge trees, it's good to keep your eyes down so the root fairies don't get you. As I looked up, I came face to face with three bear cubs be-bopping to their own beat and we all froze. The three little cubs stood on their hind legs to better examine me (or to look bigger), and looking like three cute teddies from L.L. Bean. Momma Bear, who was about 30 feet away, stiffened right up and let out a few quiet huffs. All three cubs shot up the tree in a flash. I kept my eyes on Momma, while the cubs scratched and clawed to the branches above. Their claws made enough noise that I heard them over my iPod. Then she made her move. She sat on her enormous bear-butt right in the middle of the trail.

It was like a Mexican standoff. I knew I wouldn't win so I slowly backed away. I didn't know how long the cubs would sit in the tree, so I backtracked about point-1 to wait it out. While I waited, three college-aged women approached heading towards the bears, so I told them of the situation. One of them, who had never seen a bear, insisted they go and get a picture. I recommended they wait it out a few more minutes and skip the pic, but she insisted and the others followed her. I tagged along because I thought a bear mauling would really add interest to my YouTube channel.

Actually, I went with them to protect them from their own stupidity. They were risking life and limb by disturbing a sow bear with cubs... for an Instagram shot! When we could see the bear, she had coaxed her cubs down, but when she heard the girls' high-pitched analysis, she sent them scurrying back to the safety of the branches. To emphasize her point, the Mamma Bear faced us and snapped her teeth. I'm no bearologist, but I gathered she was telling us that this portion of the trail was temporarily closed. We listened, too. Even the brave leader of the group understood "Bear."

The stand still was going on for about a half hour, and I decided to see if the trail was clear. Peeking around a tree, I could see they were gone. I turned to the girls, and they were anxiously waiting with their phones out, seemingly disappointed, when I gave them the "all clear." I cautiously proceeded keeping an eye on a brushy area to my left, when one of the girls spotted her. The excited tone of the young hiker instantly got the attention of the she-bear, and to my surprise, she rose on her hind legs to see us over the brush. It was time to back out again. She was off the trail, but as agitated as she was, it was a good idea to use caution.

The young ladies decided to head back the way they came and I decided to go around. I bushwhacked in a semicircle approximately 100 yards around the bears. I clapped my hands and spoke in a loud tone announcing myself in hopes I wouldn't meet with them – or any other bears that might be in the area. I was relieved when I got back to the trail. The visibility in the rhododendron was limited and I was jumpy. I wiped all the spider webs off my face, and moved on.

Snakes

By now, I know some of you are thinking, "I can't believe he uses his iPod on the trail. He's missing the whole experience." I thought that way, too, when I started out. Over time, and hundreds of miles, I'd heard the wilderness so much, and the trail is so repetitive, it's nice to break up that monotony with some music. Since Dusty went home, I briefly hiked with others, like EZ, but for the most part, I hiked alone and enjoyed using my iPod. But the single biggest reason for listening to music is... Rattlesnakes!

I hate snakes. All snakes. I don't care if they are cute little green snakes, harmless garter snakes, big snakes, poisonous snakes or non-poisonous snakes. It doesn't matter if they use fangs, strangulation, spit in your face, eat bugs, keep mice out of the barn or make great pets. I hate them all. Don't get me wrong, I recognize their place in the web of life, and I don't kill them. I just hate them. They just creep me out. I imagine snakes are actually where the term creepy came from. I'm also afraid of them. I don't care; call me a snake-wussy. I admit it: snakes are my kryptonite. "The rule of thumb," I've been told, "is if it has a triangle shaped head it's venomous." I don't care! They are all copper-headed, timber moccasins to me!

I bet I saw over 40 snakes on my hike! For all you snake lovers and snakeologists, fear not – snakes are alive and doing well out there. I did learn a thing or two about snakes during my time living among them. First they blend in really well. That means you don't see them until you are about to step on them. That is the precise moment they bolt for cover and scare the living crap out of you! Also, copperheads are really aggressive. Let's say for instance, you come upon a copperhead sunning itself on the trail ahead of you, do not gently nudge it with your hiking pole. Although it looks like it is in a deep sleep, it knows you are there, it feels the ground shaking, it detects your warm body and it hopes you don't see it. When you gently nudge it to clear the trail, saving yourself and all others that follow, just be aware, it will lunge remarkably far in an attempt to strike you, before your pole even touches it!

That is exactly what happened when "Teach" attempted to clear the trail for me. I was standing behind him like a child behind his mother's apron when this aggressive strike caused Teach to jump back, bumping me off the trail. I fell down on my back looking up towards my feet, which were hung up in some brush. I freaked! The last time I saw the snake, it was heading my way! Some panicky yelling went back and forth for a second or two, and then the snake caught up with the action, bolting down the hill at my side! It was no further than a foot from my face when it shot past. I nearly had a stroke!

Rattlesnakes, on the other hand, are not nearly as aggressive. They don't want to be bothered and they don't want to bother you. They even rattle to warn you where they are so you don't accidentally step on them. More snakes should have rattles. I like being the first hiker if I am hiking in a group. The first hiker arouses the snake and walks on by; the second hiker aggravates the snake; and the third gets bit. I didn't actually hear of any hikers getting bit, but that's how snakes work ... they get in your head.

I was hiking alone when I heard my first rattler. I froze. I thought it was to my left, so I took a step back and to my right. As I stepped, I checked, and sure enough, I almost stepped towards the snake. It wasn't all coiled up like in the Westerns, but it was definitely agitated, judging by the constant rattling! When I heard it, I was already past it. By stopping to locate it, I put myself in danger. My hearing seldom hinders me, but in this case it almost caused me to step on a rattler. From that day on, if I wasn't hiking with someone with two good ears, I played my music and walked down the middle of the trail.

My first good crash was at the hands of a snake (so to speak). The weather had been hot and the late spring humidity made the rocks seem like they were sweating. I had been making good time, hiking a little faster than I should have. There was a time after I lost a bunch of weight, when my conditioning was great and my legs were strong. I felt like Superman. I was descending a steep hill that ran parallel to a tumbling creek bordered with thick rhododendron and damp leaves. The huge bushes, treelike really, continued on the opposite side of the trail and climbed the hill to my right as well. I was cruising through the "Green Tunnel." With my new superpowers, I liked to challenge myself on the more technical areas without slowing down; it reminded me of skiing.

My eyes were focused on my next step, head down, planting my poles anywhere they would bite. My feet would touch and go, if the rock tipped or rolled, it didn't matter; I was off it so fast I could regain my balance on the next step or two. I was bordering on reckless. That's when I saw it; a giant snake coiled into a black pile of creepy evil! The snake must have heard me coming a mile away because he was ready for me. His head was elevated over the rest of his shiny black body, and his mouth was open in a threatening manner. I noticed it as my foot was just about to land on its big knot of coils!

The brain and body is an amazing machine. Within a nanosecond, both sides of my brain pitched in to save itself. At first glance, the left side of the brain recognized "BLACK MOMBA" and sent an alert to the rest of my body to take evasive action STAT! The left side created an option, the right side executed, and I was airborne, once again. As I was covering the distance from trail to landing zone, my left side further analyzed the reptile as a common rat snake, non-venomous, low threat. Too late. I dove about 12 feet in distance and dropped about 6 feet, crashing into the new vegetation growing up from the wet leaves that blanketed the creek-side snake habitat. Thankful I was still conscious, I scrambled back up to the trail before I checked for injuries... I felt safer on the trail.

Feeling pretty stupid, and relieved I hadn't killed myself on a rock, I went back up the hill to see this mind-altering snake. It was the biggest snake I had ever seen in the wild! It was a full six feet long with extraordinarily black blackness. It moved away in its creepy slow manner not giving me any notice. Then it did the unimaginable; it climbed into the bushes! I was mortified! The biggest advantage of sleeping in a hammock was eliminated at that moment. I watched the snake work its way to a tree and slowly climb. Its long thin body gripped the bark with ease as I watched in horror! How would I ever sleep in the forest again?

As I walked back down the hill to retrieve my poles, and gather my composure, my body was covered with goosebumps. I walked into my landing zone and was baffled to find only one pole. After a few moments, I located the other in a bush, about six feet up.

Mice

There are so many creatures out there. The most common of all are mice. Not everyone has an encounter with a moose, but everyone has a story about mice. I didn't have to deal with many mice because I seldom used the shelters, but one night, the very first night with my new pack, I had an encounter. The first pack I bought made it as far as Virginia. I lost so much weight that I couldn't tighten the waist strap enough. My make-shift solution using swimming noodles served me well, but eventually, the modification wasn't enough, and my upper straps were too big as well. I contacted the backpack company, and they replaced it with a newer and smaller pack.

I headed into the rain with my new pack, feeling like a million bucks. I stopped at a shelter to take a break from the rain and eat some food before setting out to find a campsite. Some familiar faces were there when I arrived: Red Hot, Old Eagle Scout, Walnut, Mak and Cheese, and Hasselhoff. They all had enough rain for the day and were staying there for the night. I decided to camp in the area and socialize with them, so I hung my hammock about 30 yards from the shelter. (The weather was so bad that day that Red Hot, who arrived there the previous night, took a ZERO there).

My food bag was properly hung with the others and I left my pack under my hammock for the night. A tarp was hung above the hammock to keep the rain off, and my pack was protected from the weather as well. That night, the mice, while scavenging for food, chewed a hole in my brand new pack! There was no food because I hung my foodbag from a tree, but the mice are so conditioned to look for food in packs, they searched mine anyway.

Coyotes

While coyotes are a rare sight, they are in abundance in the Appalachian woods. The high-pitch howl that excites the response of the pack is an eerie sound that pierces the night woods. The lead singer starts howling its solo and is then joined by its band in a crescendo of frenzied yips and long howls. The performance is usually repeated a few times, each from a slightly different location, allowing you to follow their movements. Sometimes, when the howling seems to stop moving, I wonder if they've had a successful hunt.

One June evening in Pennsylvania, I was sitting on a high overlook, enjoying the view and zoning out, when Red Hot came hiking up the trail. By now, he and I had bumped into each other several times along the trail and we got along pretty well. Talking away like fellow New Englanders tend to, we sat on those rocks until the sun went down. I hiked with him to the next shelter where we parted and I went to find a place to stealth camp. The trail turned and headed down the mountain, and it was thick with brush on both sides. I hiked down for about 40 minutes before I found a break in the foliage. I set my hammock deeper in the woods than normal, just to get through the brush. I stuck a pole in the ground, marking my way back to the trail in the morning, and set up my hammock. Within minutes I was asleep.

(Whenever I set up a camp in the dark, I look forward to seeing it in the morning. Once, I was camped in a quiet little meadow feeling like I might be the first person that ever stepped foot there. When I looked at my phone to check for cell service, I was shocked to see I was getting a Wi-Fi signal from a nearby house!)

This site wasn't at the bottom of the mountain, but it leveled off nicely and as far as my headlight beam shown, it was relatively open. After midnight the unmistakable sound of a pack of coyotes broke the silence with a chorus of howls and yips. They were close, but it's hard to tell; their sound travels a long way. A few minutes later they sounded off again, much closer. Even with my poor skills at locating sounds, I could tell they were heading my way. It is uncommon for a human to be attacked by a coyote – the occasional domestic pet or small child, maybe – but rarely a full-sized human. I continued to lie in my hammock, waiting for the next song to update their whereabouts.

Before long I could hear the forest come alive with the sounds of the running animals. Their paws landing on the damp leaves sounded like the happy trotting of Springer Spaniels hunting quail. I was straining to try to pin-point them when the sounds stopped. I don't know how many were out there, but they must have smelled me, and for the moment, the hair on the back of my neck stood. Like a trumpet blast, they all sounded off! I could feel the sound shaking my chest like I was standing in front of a speaker! I tried to remain calm despite my predicament, relying on my position at the top of the food chain to save me. I took my headlight out, leaned out of my hammock and swept it around while yelling. I saw three sets of yellowish gold eyes to my right and flashes of two others a little further out. My yelling seemed to bring the revelry to an end, but they cautiously walked around before running off.

I'm certain they weren't hunting me – I was probably hanging in their path of travel. When they came upon me, they must have thought I was a giant burrito hanging there. I didn't get much sleep that night. My adrenalin was still squirting out of my ears when the sky turned light gray, just before sunrise.

Not all encounters with wildlife are as dramatic as the bear, snakes and coyotes. The little dwellers are ever present. Before you put your shoes on in the morning, it's good to pick the spiders out. Squirrels are cute, but if you don't cinch your pack up when you camp, you may be surprised when you unpack 20 miles later and Tamiasciurus Hudsonicus leaps to freedom. I never saw a big millipede until I went on this hike, but after flicking a thousand of them off my ground sheet, I'm good. There is no getting the gunk out of your clothes when you sit on a slug, and your heart feels like you ran over a dog when you accidentally step on a newt.

Ruffed grouse will scare you to near heart failure when they break cover in an explosion of wings and leaves. Turkeys will wake you up before dawn in April and May with their thundering gobbles, which will be about three hours after a whip-poor-will is done announcing his territory with a marathon of breathless calls. The big bullfrogs will croak relentlessly near ponds and swamps, but the spring peepers seem to be everywhere. At least snapping turtles don't make noise.

Only one of nature's creatures can cause depression, excitement, awe, frustration and hunger. You can plan to encounter them when you are standing on a suspension bridge deep in the woods, looking into a clear deep pool, without a rod: Trout. When I finished my hike, I spent the winter dreaming of those trout. I drove back down south to fish them in the spring.

Incidentally, I have no moose stories.

Boardwalk in New Jersey

16

Closing in on New England

I left Pennsylvania feeling like I had just been in a fight. I had fallen behind my bubble, was physically exhausted and mentally fried. To add insult to injury, the rain accompanied me to the state line insuring my misery to my last step. My hopes of smoother trails on the far banks of the Delaware River would wait to be seen. I was taking a badly needed ZERO.

It was the fourth of July and Steve, my brother-in-law, picked me up on the far side of the bridge, squeezing his car between the highway and the guardrails. We headed to his home where I was overjoyed to see my sister and her family. The long hike and my recent struggles were taking me on an emotional rollercoaster, and seeing their faces threatened to break those emotions wide open. I managed to keep everything under control, but I hadn't realized how badly I was missing parts of my real life. My nieces and nephews had never seen me with a beard or so skinny, so I was quite a spectacle.

We had a wonderful picnic, complete with friends, food and a campfire. My niece, Elise, pointed to the horizon where we could see the High Point Monument, a huge obelisk that I would be hiking past in the next day or two. (The trail was always right there.) The time I spent with my family was exactly what I needed to recharge my batteries and get my head right before heading back out in the morning.

Steve and my nephew, Jared, brought me back to the Delaware Water Gap and joined me on the trail for a few miles before heading back. I was disappointed to see that the rocks didn't end at the river, but hiking together made it fun. I was wearing my third pair of new hiking shoes, the sun was out, and Steve stopped in plenty of time when a rattlesnake slithered across the trail. Life was good again.

We took a break near Sunfish Pond. I ate a tuna tortilla while they snacked on power bars. Before long, we said our good byes and headed in opposite directions.

I like New Jersey. The stone covered ridges wound through low growing brush and offered views from the occasional fire tower. The grass-covered meadows look like parks and the low lands have elaborate boardwalks leading through the swamps.

The Garden State lives up to its name. On one occasion when I was enjoying trail magic, the Angels informed me that the fresh tomatoes, peppers, lettuce and cukes were fresh from their gardens. There was a common rumor that New Jersey stinks. Let me be the first to tell you... it's true. At first I was defensive; after all, my sister lives there. Having hiked 72 miles through the state I learned why. The giant swamps are in a constant cycle of growth and decay. When hiking through the state, the trail spends a lot of time in these swamps, utilizing boardwalks and bog bridges. Some of them are pretty ripe.

Although this can be unpleasant to your olfactory senses, I assure you swamps just plain stink... It's not just New Jersey.

"Lean To"

New Jersey lends about 70 miles to the trail, and somewhere towards the northern end I met up with "Lean To." He and I had been leap-frogging since Tennessee so we were well-acquainted by the time we hit New Jersey. His wide-brimmed hat, bushy beard, huge pack and well-worn shirt with an upside down canoe were a familiar sight; he looked like the quintessential thru-hiker. I liked him right away. He is a talker. He can talk while he hikes. He talks when he climbs, when he descends, in the morning, noon or night. He can strike up a conversation with a rock. He also has an unlimited amount of trivia bouncing around in his head. (I called him Cliff Clavin, a character in the '80s TV series *Cheers*.) We talked about the trail, the weather, our gear, politics, family... and snakes. (He doesn't like snakes either.)

Lean To and I would spend the next 100 miles hiking together. By the time we hit the New York line I was feeling much better than when I was in Pennsylvania. The protein drinks, trips for town food and all the fresh veggies were doing the trick. The trail was never far from civilization, so there was always a diner nearby. (New Jersey has nice diners.) They don't allow hitch-hiking in that state, so I had to keep an eye out for the law. Getting a ride was just as easy there though. (It seems that wherever the trail passes, regardless which state, the locals remain hiker-friendly.) With all the trips to eat, I was gaining some weight back and feeling stronger than ever.

Lean To and I were unlikely hiking partners. He was well-organized and was familiar with the trail long before we passed through an area. In contrast, I seldom looked at my map; as long as I could find the next blazed tree I was good. We hiked at different speeds so I slowed up a little and he sped up a little. I would zip up a hill, eat an energy bar, and Lean To would be along shortly after, picking up the conversation exactly where it had left off at the bottom. Other times, I would go ahead and he would follow behind listening to a podcast. He would catch up and summarize the podcast for me... whether I wanted to hear it or not.

Despite our hiking differences, we crossed into New York where we managed to stay together through some of my favorite parts of the trail thus far. The terrain was changing drastically. Instead of the monotony of small rocks in Pennsylvania, the rocks structures, like the Lemon Squeezer, the old stone shelters and dramatic climbs were building my excitement for what was to come in New England.

New York had some of the most impressive stone work I had experienced since beginning my hike, and I was amazed at the quality. It's common to have a short stretch of neatly constructed trail with fancy stone steps and sometimes paved or graveled walkways near trailheads. The closer to urban areas, the nicer these trailheads seem to be. In most cases they only last a short way, point-2 or so. If you parked your car at one of these trailheads, you would think the whole trail is smooth and friendly. Really it's a tease. I was certain the improved areas were designed to trick you into hiking. Soon the well-groomed surface narrows, leading you into the woods and the "real trail." I like discovering these manicured stretches; they announce a road crossing... and possibly a nearby diner.

We hiked within 30 miles of New York City where over 20 million people live, yet, the trail passed quietly by, offering few views of the cultural and financial capital of the world. Lights could be seen at night, and glimpses of the Hudson River and its busy shores were visible from the Perkins Memorial Tower atop Bear Mountain, but the trail held on to its rugged remote feel.

The trail did offer a taste of civilization when we passed through the Bear Mountain State Park, however, a popular destination for those city dwellers looking to spend time outdoors. Trail construction crews have built the most amazing stone steps leading into and out of that area. When we came down the north side of the mountain we were delivered into a park full of weekend picnickers and the smells of the food they brought with them. Hundreds of families gathered along the shore of a small pond, listening to music and lounging in the shade of the huge oak trees. It was like traveling through "It's a Small World" exhibit at Disney World. There was Spanish music, reggae, rap, rock, Indian music and country. Each music genre was accompanied by matching mouthwatering aromas like Spanish rice, jerk chicken and American barbecue. It was murder! By the time Lean To and I passed through, we were so hungry we went straight to a barbecue joint and devoured large portions of some unlucky farm animal.

We headed out over the Bear Mountain Bridge where I stood midway between the shores of the Hudson River, waiting for Lean To. For a half hour, I watched freight trains and barges haul cargo through the valley. Lean To, having found a Mountain Dew machine, happily hiked his way along the pedestrian walkway, sipping his soda. He was brimming to tell me about his daring six-lane crossing to the soda machine. Between the crowded park fiesta, a tour of the Bear Mountain Zoo (the trail passed right through), and the hustle and bustle of the bridge traffic, I was anxious to get back into the mountains on the other side of the river. He would have to talk and walk... and he did.

Crossing the Hudson was a big deal for me. Up until now I felt like I was simply traveling north. Being a New Englander, we proudly refer to ourselves as being from the Northeast. When I crossed that river, I felt like I was heading home. If I continued north, I would head up to the Adirondack Mountains; therefore, the trail turns northeast to

Maine. It felt as though I had turned on to my street. I was starting to feel the pull from "The Greatest Mountain."

Eager to get into Connecticut, I was hiking with a new vigor. I was back in peak form, my knee braces (two now) were keeping my knees together, I continued to regain weight and my energy was back. The trail was interesting, beautiful and challenging. The weather was hot but rain free, and the blueberries were ripe... There was nothing stopping me!

I found myself leaving Lean To behind more and more, which he didn't mind; he liked to listen to podcasts. I would get to the top of a mountain and eat, or update my social media, and he would be along like a reliable mailman. Sometimes he would hike on by and I'd catch up to him later on. We were both snake-jumpy so we liked having two sets of eyes on the trail. That's another thing about snakes, when you see one, every stick, root and vine you see for the next 24 hours makes you jump!

We started up a long climb, which Lean To already spotted on his map. I decided to go ahead, have some lunch and maybe take a nap. He was listening to someone's conspiracy theories on his iPod, so we agreed to meet up later. I found a comfy spot about 20 yards off the trail and before long I saw him hiking up the hill. I called to him a couple of times to no avail; he was deep into the podcast. I wasn't done with my siesta yet, so I decided to toss a stick in front of him to get his attention.

I whipped it side-armed so it would skip through the leaves; after all, I didn't want to hit him. Accidentally, or maybe unconsciously, my aim was off by a few degrees. The stick bounced off the leaves like a skipped rock on a calm pond, and came to a tumbling stop at his feet. The quick motion of the stick in the brown leaves, along with the sudden noise, resembled a timber rattler to his snake-jumpy brain. Lean To jumped straight up, twisted 45 degrees, and landed with both poles and both feet simultaneously! His poles stretched out to stab the attacking snake while his feet stretched way back to avoid a strike! It looked like a panicked cross-fit move! The sound that escaped him was so dire I instantly regretted throwing the stick! When I saw the look of sheer panic on his face I immediately jumped to my feet and started begging for forgiveness!

When I stood, he began to process what had just happened. A few seconds later when he regained his wits, we fell into a fit of laughter that would last about 10 minutes. He swore revenge, but held no ill feelings. We still fall into fits of uncontrolled laughter when we talk about it! Two weeks after my return from the trail I received an envelope in the mail with no return address. Without looking, I reached in and was terrified when I grabbed a fake snake. His revenge was swift.

Between the laughs, stories and trivia, Lean To and I managed to work our way through the 90 miles of New York. He was especially interested in Nuclear Lake; with the many "theories" regarding its name, it was right up his alley. We continued to drift apart during the day but he always managed to find me at the end of the day. When he did, he would always seem to have a Yogi story... as in the cartoon character Yogi Bear; he was the king of "Yogi-ing." While we were separated he would meet people, strike up a rapport with them, and before long they would be offering food, water or liquor. Unlike Trail Angels, they had no intentions of conducting this act of kindness. They would become hypnotized by his charm and offer to help... or something like that. Once he managed to get a pack full of dehydrated meals from a family who was getting off the trail! For him it was an art to "yogi." I felt there was a fine line between "yogi-ing" and begging. Rule of thumb: It's okay to "yogi"... as long as you don't ask.

17

Back Home in Connecticut

I was excited to cross the Connecticut line, so excited that I hiked 24 miles that day. It was a mellow hike through a mild section of trail, and Lean To managed to hang in there with me, sharing my enthusiasm. We had the pleasure of crossing over with China Rock, who we had been hiking with throughout the day. She, too, had a high-mileage day, but enjoyed the milestone with us before moving on. I was entering my home state; she was leaving hers.

The three of us stopped for pictures at the green sign noting "The Gateway to New England," and once again I found myself a little choked up with emotion. Stepping foot into my home state felt amazing. It had been months since I left – and a lifetime of hiking – but here I was, standing in the Nutmeg State. To my west I knew no one. To my east, all the way to Cape Cod, lived every friend, former coworker and relative I've known for years. With a phone call, I could leave the trail and never return.

Connecticut isn't that big. It's only 110 miles from east to west and 70 miles from south to north. Just over 50 miles of the AT call Connecticut home, and it travels through the northwest corner. Being from the northeast corner where the hills roll and the agricultural fields line the country roads, I was surprised to see how strenuous the terrain was. The huge stone ledges and rugged elevation gains were a huge contrast to the mild hills to the east. One of the most treacherous descents thus far was St. Johns Ledges. Although it would seem mild compared to the challenges ahead in the coming weeks, it was as steep and rugged as anything since the beginning of my hike. For perspective, it is a popular place for rock climbers to play.

When Lean To and I were making our slow descent over the large boulders and man-made steps, we came across a woman who was having a bad day. Her name was "Scientist," and she was a solo, long-distance section-hiker. She was no newcomer to the trail and had logged over a thousand miles thus far, but she was stuck. When we found her she was sitting on a steep-angled slab of rock, with her pack off, and visibly shaken. She couldn't go up and couldn't go down. When she looked up to Lean To and I, it looked like she was ready for a full-blown breakdown.

We could see she was having troubles, so we stopped. After a little chit chat, I took her pack and Lean To talked her down the ledges. He pointed out footholds and handholds, and held her hand when she slid on her butt. It took about 45 minutes, but she made it to the bottom. She was a little butt-sore and her ego was bruised, but other than that we left her in a cheery mood.

Scott

When we got to the bottom of St. Johns Ledges, the most difficult descent since beginning, my lifelong buddy, Scott, arrived to bring me to his home for a meal, soft bed and laundry. After hiking over 100 miles together, Lean To and I would part ways. Knowing how the trail works, we were confident we would meet again, so we bumped fists and headed off on our separate ways.

Scott, my childhood partner-in-crime and all things adventurous, brought me to his home where his wife Christine and daughter Lorna rolled out the red carpet. We ate a delicious meal, sat around the table like civilized folk, and he even bought me my favorite fancy beer, Miller Lite. If I knew this was the way I would be treated, I would have hiked the trail years ago!

We talked the night away, discussing books, our recent retirement (he recently retired from the Connecticut State Police), politics and the good old days. This, of course, defeated the purpose of a trail pick-up, but because he lived on the western side of the state, we never seem to get together enough anyway. By the time we hit the sack it was closer to morning than it was to midnight, so we slept late. He had been watching my videos and knew my penchant for germ-free environments, so he assured me all the sheets and pillowcases were clean. This was especially funny because when we were kids, he'd squirt milk into my mouth straight from the cow, during chores. (I guess germ-consciousness is a learned behavior.) He tried my backpack on for size, which I left out on the porch, and promptly threw his shirt in the wash. (I guess he wasn't used to "trail aromas.")

Before bringing me back to the trail with my sweet-smelling clothes all washed and some KT tape for my knees, we went to a diner for breakfast. The hot coffee helped clear the fog of an all-nighter, and the food was icing to the meal Scott and Christine treated me to the night before. I could've spent a few more days there, and they offered, but I was adamant to get back. We drank a couple more cups of coffee then headed to the trail. I hated to go.

The next couple miles of trail were easy, following the bank of the Housatonic River, and I found myself scuffing along like a kid who didn't want to go home. Physically I was fine, but seeing my close friends, and knowing I was no longer walking toward my home, but away from it, was having a weird effect on me. I had hiked for months with that feeling of walking home – it was my driving force. The Greatest Mountain, Katahdin, my ultimate goal, was still over 600 miles away. I was hiking alone again and I couldn't shake the feeling that I was now walking away from everything I knew.

The trail held distractions from my somber mood, however, I couldn't stay blue while walking through the open fields, wooded forests and small towns of my home state; it was beautiful. At one point, due to a detour, I hiked past Lime Rock Park, a racetrack, where I could hear the cars ripping around the course. I decided to go in. Unfortunately, it's closed to the public. I noticed the business office, went in, and requested a tour. After talking to Mike, the head of security, he offered to take me around. We spent the next two hours driving around the track, visiting the driving school and touring the pits. Mike was patient, answered all my questions and showed me some incredible cars. He ended the tour though, when I attempted to "yogi" some pulled pork at a private function held on the grounds. Despite my faux pas, he brought me back to the business office where I could resume my hike.

It isn't uncommon along the trail that you walk on asphalt, or sidewalks, to get through a town or around a detour. Like Hot Springs, North Carolina, Damascus, Virginia, and Duncannon, Pennsylvania, the trail in Connecticut had a stretch which leads along the country roads for a few miles. It was one of these stretches, where my entire hike would change... only I didn't know it.

I was alone click-clacking the titanium tips of my trekking poles up a hill along a rural road. I was swatting the incessant mosquitoes which had been plaguing me since northern New York, when I saw a hiker sitting on a bench. From a distance I knew who it was right away. His tall narrow frame, red neckerchief and telltale green "Maine" hat was unmistakable. It was Red Hot.

The bench was near the road in front of a retirement community where seniors can sit and watch the traffic. Red Hot was talking on his phone, taking a break in the shade, when I called out to him. He ended his call, jumped up and met me on the road as I approached. It was good to see him again; the last time was in Pennsylvania, at the buffet. We sat on the bench, catching up, like we did on the rock overlook before the coyote incident. He had been hiking alone for a while and we decided to move out together.

Running low on water, he told me to keep an eye out for a source, so I did. In fact, we strolled up to one of the senior living units and filled up out of a spigot. It looked suspicious, two grown men hiding behind the bushes, but mission accomplished, and we were on our way.

Before long we were running through cornfields like two kids on summer vacation, and laughing at each other's jokes. The hiking became effortless again and we were closing in on Massachusetts. We blasted up Bear Mountain and sat atop a large rock cairn, drying our sweat soaked shirts in the breeze. Shark Bait from Massachusetts joined us while we ate a snack, and we each mentally checked off another state line. The last time I saw Shark Bait was in New Jersey, where we shared a ride to a diner for breakfast and coffee. The mental lift of crossing into another state never loses its power; in fact, it gets stronger. We were flying high.

We decided to find a place to camp within the next hour or so, so we took off. Within a few hundred yards, maybe point-1, I crashed. I didn't fall; I was hit with a wave of nausea. The 90 degree heat had gotten to me. I began sweating profusely, my legs went weak and I needed to puke. I told Red Hot that I wasn't feeling well, and that I was going to take another break. Fully expecting him to move on and find a campsite, he told me that the same thing was happening to him! We stopped and sat on a clear area of rock slabs and took off our packs.

We remained there quietly recovering from what we were sure was heat exhaustion for the next half hour. We realized that we were surrounded by thousands of ripe blueberries, so we spent the next twenty minutes gathering and eating ourselves back to health. It was now almost an hour closer to dark and we decided to camp at the next good spot.

Soon we found ourselves following a ravine into a hemlock forest with a brook stair-stepping its way through it. Each small waterfall held a shallow pool and you couldn't even get near them without being engulfed with mosquitoes! The pine needles blanketing the ground were damp under the thick canopy, which also blocked much of the daylight, creating an early twilight effect. We had just crossed into

Massachusetts and we were ready to camp. Red Hot and I decided to cross the mosquito breeding-pools, and camp on a relatively flat area on the other side. We set up close to the brook, so the sound of the water would drown out the constant buzz of the flying bloodsuckers.

Two things disrupt a normal camp routine: bad weather and mosquitoes. Being well-practiced, we both had our camps set quickly; he used a tent and I hung my hammock. The hungry insects boldly risked being crushed for a sip of blood, and many were successful. I applied 100% DEET like it was sunscreen, set up my hammock, then washed the DEET all off before climbing in to eat in the protection of a bug net. Red Hot ate outside of his tent because it was the size of a tube sock, burning the shrink wrap from his dehydrated food in an attempt to keep the bugs away. He opted for toxic smoke rather than the mosquitoes.

Fire-and-Ice, from New Hampshire, and Fonzie camped by the brook, but due to the mosquitoes, we didn't see them after their tents were set up. The babbling from the small waterfall was welcome company because everyone, even those who don't camp, knows how hypnotizing that sound is.

My time with Red Hot was short lived because the next day we came upon trail magic when we came out of the woods. The Trail Angels were none other than Red Hot's two daughters, Lily and Ali! They drove out to cook their Dad a steak and feed hikers a buffet that would rival any Fourth of July party in America. I enjoyed some food and drinks before leaving Red Hot with his daughters for some family time, but before I left there were already 20 hikers eating dogs and sauerkraut, beans and beer.

I hated to leave Red Hot behind. He and I had a lot in common, mostly though, he was a happy guy and a fellow New Englander. Like Dusty, we hit it off. Great Barrington wasn't far away and I wanted to post a video, so I left him behind to enjoy his girls. I knew he missed them.

I made it to the road where, if I was lucky, I could hitch into town for the night. Of all the time I spent on the trail, the last few hundred feet to the road leading to Great Barrington was the most mosquito-infested land I had traveled! I managed to catch a ride with a stoner whose car smelled like Cheech and Chong's car, but it was better than getting eaten alive! Within a few miles he dropped me off at a motel, and soon after, I was checked in. It would be the most expensive motel I stayed at on my trip.

The town of Great Barrington was nice. I walked around and ate ice cream, headed to the laundry mat. After my clean clothes were stuffed back into my backpack, I strolled around the town, but it was small and I saw it all in an hour. I then bought a burrito and headed back to my room where I took a shower, ate my food and posted a new video. There were a few new hikers there that I hadn't met, but they had seen my vids and treated me very nice. I caught a few hours of sleep, checked out, grabbed a coffee and a couple apples from the lobby and caught a ride back to the trail with a soccer mom in a light blue minivan. My whole Great Barrington stop had cost me almost 200 bucks with food, room and a Dr. Pepper. That equated to about 20 bucks an hour. Not a cheap stop!

"Simple Man" and Family

Every time I posted a video, I wondered what interesting people or trail features I would find for the next video, so I always had my eyes open. I didn't have to wait long. The day was much more pleasant than the previous – mid 80s, light breeze and mosquito free. I was hiking with Simple Man from Dallas, Texas, and we were making good time as we passed the miles in light conversation. Simple Man was thru-hiking the trail with his wife Chocolate, daughter Lollipop and sons Dash, Turbo, Tigger and Mud Magnet. They ranged from 9 to 17, and they started in Georgia two weeks after I had. We crossed paths for the first time in Connecticut, the day my friend Scott returned me to the trail. I'm sure they would have passed me somewhere in Pennsylvania had they not taken every Sunday off to honor the Sabbath.

Simple Man and I were approaching a narrow walking bridge that crossed over a thick swamp when we heard screaming, real pain-filled screaming. Simple Man calmly said, "That's one of mine." And we ran towards his kids who were ahead on the twisting bridge, out of sight. The whole bridge wiggled and shook as we ran two feet above the aquatic vegetation and pockets of still water. The tall saplings of swamp maple and birch limited our view to a few yards and it seemed we'd never find them. My mind was trying to guess what dangers lurked that would result in such a scream? Then, we almost ran headlong into Tigger and Mud Magnet, who were running back towards us in a panicked sprint. We barely got out of the way as the boys blew past us on the narrow swamp-bridge yelling, "BEEEES!"

We caught up to them on the edge of the swamp where the bridge ended to assess the damage. Mud Magnet, the nine year old, with possibly the smallest head of any hiker on the trail, got two stings on top of it. (Don't misunderstand me; he has a normal-sized head, for a nine year old.) Tigger was unscathed. Mud Magnet took it like a champ, (better than most adults I know), and Tigger quickly rebounded from the shock of hearing his little brother scream a mixture of pain and terror. Simple Man, disaster averted, was already formulating a plan to get past the bees.

The boys described the swarm as three feet in size and coming from the wooden slats of the swamp bridge. I wanted to reconnoiter, but Simple Man, the leader of all things spiritual and dangerous,

Lean To

decided we'd go for it. We all dug out our rain gear for self-preservation and prepared to shoot through the swarm. Yes, we knew there would be casualties, but there was no other option. The moment before we began our charge, Tigger said, "Shouldn't we leave a note or something for the other hikers?" His compassion for others at that moment is something I'll never forget.

I wrote a note on a piece of paper, placed it on the bridge with a rock, and we lined up like a SWAT door-entry team and began creeping forward. Our group had grown to five and I took point position. I'm not that gallant; I just couldn't miss the opportunity to document this for next week's video. As we got close to the swarm, Simple Man told me to start running so I did. The bridge was rocking and creaking with the concussions of 10 pounding feet which was like a bomb siren from the '50s, sending all available bees to defend the fortress. When I saw them, the swarm was indeed three feet, covering the bridge from side to side and equally as high; they were mad... and ready!

I poured it on and ran straight down the plank walkway cutting the swarm in half. I could feel contact from about a dozen bees, but remarkably I was only stung once! Everyone was yelling from their stings and there was a moment of chaos when I failed to notice the bridge turned slightly to my right. I continued on my original path of travel until gravity took over... I ran off the bridge.

It was a fast soft landing, enabling me to roll a couple times before sinking my feet in the soft mud. By the time I got back to the bridge, there were only one or two people who hadn't passed me. I actually think I heard Simple Man laughing as he ran by! We all stopped running on the far side where Eight Paws and Laces were licking their wounds from their passage, moments before we arrived. Eight Paws was a cute canine-hiker who was with her two trail humans, Clover and M&M from Cape Cod. Laces took a nasty sting on her lip which swelled to impressive proportions. Sting count: 8 out of 13 hikers.

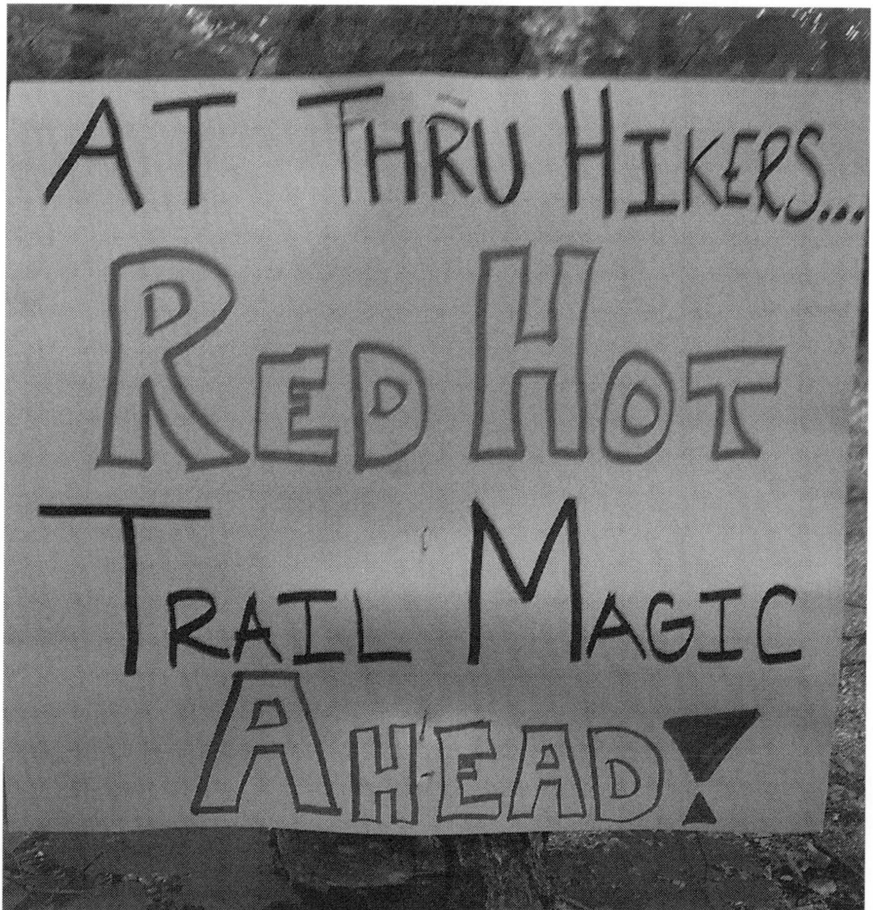
AT THRU HIKERS...
RED HOT
TRAIL MAGIC
AHEAD!

18

In the ZONE

I had been waiting for this day for a while. My friend Donny was meeting me on the trail for a few miles and of all the people I knew, he was the one person who understood what I was doing out there. Donny and I had been coworkers at the prison and over time had become good friends. If we weren't sitting in patrol vehicles outside the fence talking about family or the forests, we were conducting tactical training with the Connecticut's elite emergency response team. He is a man's man: courageous prison guard, mountaineer, mountain rescue volunteer and family man.

Like most of my friends, I hadn't seen Donny in a while. He had been very supportive, keeping in touch with me regularly throughout my hike. Hiking a few miles in our element was something we had been talking about for months. We spoke in the morning and agreed on a place to meet. He parked his van at a trailhead and hiked in a few miles. Unfortunately, the bee incident set me back a little and I had no phone service to let him know I was running a little late. He waited over an hour and turned back.

When I reached the trailhead where he was parked, he told me what happened and said that he had just returned to his van. Essentially, I followed him out, trailing him point-2 behind all the way! It was a great visit. We sat on the grass and talked away for an hour, just like we did when we parked in the shade of the guard towers at the prison. The time flew by and family responsibilities required his presence, but before he left, he opened the back doors to his van and completely resupplied me for my next section – including a fresh new can of Skoal.

During Donny's visit, several hikers walked out of the woods and crossed the dirt road where he was parked. We could hear them poling away on the wood planks that stretched over the swampy wetland. They each lit up at the sight of Donny's van thinking it was trail magic. The hikers would quickly realize it was a mirage – just a parked vehicle – and hike on, deflated. (Trail magic was no longer a pleasant surprise; it had become expected.) A few hikers I knew would stop long enough for me to introduce my friend, visit and then continue on.

Donny and I said our good-byes, complete with man-hug, and I began to leave. Hearing the distinct sound of hiking poles on wood, I turned to see who I'd be hiking with. To my surprise, out of the woods came none other than the neckerchief-wearing, tall-framed, green-hatted... Red Hot! Donny, who recognized him from my videos, stayed for a few minutes longer and welcomed Red to Massachusetts with some resupplies.

Red Hot thanked me for the note on the bridge. He had managed to sneak by without being stung a - tactic I should've tried. We were on the cusp of The Berkshires, or at least that's what the sign said when we crossed the Mass Pike, the main interstate from Boston to Albany, New York. We took a few minutes on the pedestrian bridge before moving on. We both knew the bridge well, having driven under it hundreds of times between us. Despite being in Massachusetts, it was the exact place on the trail that was closest to my home. I was feeling the pull of The Greatest Mountain, it was stronger than the pull towards home, and so Red and I crossed the bridge and continued towards Maine.

I was still in familiar territory, and despite being stung a couple hours earlier, it would continue to be one of those days I'd remember forever. On the north side of the Mass Pike, my close friend Paul was picking me up and taking me home for the night. Paul is the kind of friend that no matter where you are or what you are doing, you come away with memories, a sore gut from laughing and selfies that usually have dead animals or fish in them. He's the kind of friend that would come anywhere or anytime if called. I called. This time, however, I wouldn't be leaving the trail alone; Red Hot was coming, too.

When we arrived at his home nestled at the bottom of the Berkshire Mountains, we were greeted by one of my dearest friends, Joe. Paul's brother. Over the years, we have spent more time together in the woods, or standing on frozen lakes, than we spent indoors - poker games excluded. I was so happy to see their wives and their adult children; they are like family. I can't possibly describe these friends to you. I'll sum it up by saying that the world is a better place because of each of them.

Red Hot was welcomed into Paul and Cecile's home like one of the family, and we were led to the dining room where we couldn't believe our eyes! Spread out in a formal place setting was a feast. Before us was a giant platter of venison, pasta salad, garden salad, wine, bread... everything. Red Hot and I stared in disbelief and I heard him whisper, "Holy cats!"

Their hospitality was amazing. We ate like kings, our clothes were washed – some replaced. Joe treated me to Miller Lite and after supper we all sat around the fire pit watching a meteor shower late into the night. When we settled in for the night in the rec room, Red Hot looked at me and said, "I guess I ran into you just in time."

We were up at 6 a.m. with boots on the trail by 7. The next couple days we managed to get our momentum back. We both had been getting spoiled with trail magic lately, and our mileage had suffered. We made a plan to remain on the trail and keep moving towards Vermont. Red Hot and I were getting to know each other better, and I learned that he was easy to talk into a diner stop. We stopped twice for breakfast in the next two days; we were going to get along fine. We agreed that our decision to remain on-trail didn't apply to diner stops.

By the time we arrived in North Adams, Massachusetts, we were getting excited to cross into Vermont. Nothing short of cardiac arrest would stop us from stepping foot into State #12 before we camped. We were on a mission. We followed the white blazes through town, looking forward to getting off the hot sidewalk and into the fast approaching Green Mountains.

That is when we ran into my good friend Pauly. Pauly and I worked together in corrections and he is an avid hiker. Many of the trail-miles I hiked to get here, he had already hiked. His daughter was holding a

Paul, one of my biggest supporters

colorful handmade "Trail Magic" sign in case we didn't see the giant bald guy sitting in the shade on the side of the sidewalk.

He was one of my biggest supporters. He often called or messaged me, encouraging me, and pumping me up as I worked my way north. He told me he would try to catch me when I passed through Massachusetts, but I was losing hope as I got closer to Vermont. Just a few miles from the border, he parked under a white blaze, and watched that sidewalk until Red Hot and I came by.

Pauly calls me Sammy. In fact, most of my close friends from the prison do. I hope it is a term of endearment, but for whatever reason, Red Hot had heard it a few times in the last few days. He asked me if I was part of a bald Mafia or something. I didn't get it. He said he was suspicious about getting trail magic from a Donny, Joey, and a Pauly, each bald, calling me Sammy, and each claiming to be a prison guard! I told him to "fugetaboutit."

Pauly resupplied Red Hot and I completely. He knew what to bring, our food bags were stuffed; we wouldn't have to stop again for a week. More hikers arrived, then more behind them. Within an hour there were twenty hikers sitting on the grass in front of the elementary school. Pauly brought enough for everyone.

Pauly isn't a drinker, but he is thoughtful. Due to the hot summer day, he thought Red Hot and I would be thirsty for a couple cold beers. We were, indeed. Naturally, the first one was cold and refreshing, leading to the next, and so on... I am not much of a drinker to begin with, but due to factors unknown to me, I went from lightweight to ultra-lightweight. Thanks to Pauly, we wouldn't be walking into Vermont today.

Three hours later and back on the trail, Red Hot and I crossed the creepy Blair Witch Bridge on the edge of town, leading into the woods, and decided to camp early rather than stumble our way to Vermont. The bright yellow bridge had thousands of painted handprints on it. It looked like the bridge of doom.

We managed to stumble up the hill leading into the woods and find a place to camp about 100 yards off the trail. We set our tent and hammock about 20 yards apart and escaped the mosquitoes by retreating inside our rig. The nylon walls and mesh that protected us from hungry insects didn't hamper our ability to converse, so we reflected on the last week. We received trail magic from his family and my friends four times, and probably gained five pounds each! The last thing I heard him say before we fell asleep was, "We are in the zone."

We were fast asleep before dark. We blamed our lack of motivation and impaired coordination on the heat.

Around midnight something woke me up. It took a few seconds to remember where I was – all the campsites kind of blend together after a while. I strained my ears to hear what it was, and for a minute or so it was silent. Our camp was a level patch of woods surrounded with green vegetation. There was no campfire ring, no logs to sit on, just low brush and a carpet of leaves. The leaves were fluffy and dry, and above us was a lush canopy of maple branches, laden with next year's carpet.

Staring into the darkness, I heard a very distinctive sound of something running in the woods. That wasn't uncommon. After a while, normal woodland sounds don't even make it past your subconscious. This was different. The first thing I noticed was that it was fast... and close! The sounds it made as it ran in the crunchy leaves were loud enough to track its movements. I would hear it coming for five seconds or so, before it ran right past our camp and then beyond.

I've spent a large portion of my life in the woods. In all my hours of sitting in a tree waiting for a deer, calling turkeys and checking trap lines, I thought I knew every creature in the woods. I racked my brain trying to figure it out, but was coming up blank. I leaned out of my hammock with my headlight in my hand and tried to see this ground missile when it ran by, but after several fly-bys I still hadn't seen it. It was time to wake Red Hot.

"Hey."

"What?"

"Do you hear that?"

"Yeah, what is it?"

"I don't know... here it comes again..."

I was searching with my light, and because of my poor hearing, Red was helping me with coordinates.

Red: "Did you see it?"

"No"

"It sounds like a person."

It did! Whatever it was had a distinctive two foot sound – a biped. I ruled out turkeys – not their behavior. Not bear – they rarely travel upright. Not a cat, coon, fisher, bird or beast – I was stumped. Whatever it was, it was elusive. My mind was rifling through back episodes of National Geographic. Soon I was imagining little invisible trolls running through the forest (Maybe it was the creepy bridge).

"It hit my tent!"

"Was it big?"

"No. "

Then I saw it. It ran smack dab into my backpack a foot from my face! In the beam of my headlamp I saw a creature I had never seen before. It rolled following its impact, giving me a good view. It looked like a large mouse, smaller than a common rat, Maybe three and a half inches long, with large haunches, long rear legs, large feet and a long tail. It instantly sprung into the darkness and was gone. The little furry brown rodent reminded me of Speedy Gonzalez, the cartoon character.

For the next hour, Red Hot and I were subject to dozens of flybys. We didn't know if it was the same one or a whole colony. They were driving us crazy. The long leaps continued to sound like little running trolls, and sleep was impossible. We tried yelling but that didn't faze them. I got up and tried throwing sticks as they hopped past like bionic miniature kangaroos. It didn't help. Finally, after lying in my hammock enduring the forest version of Chinese water torture, I hooted.

I had heard hundreds of owls in the last few months, so I did my best impression. I sucked a lungful of air and let out my best, "Whoo.. whoo... whoo cooks for you...." Problem solved! We didn't hear another Woodland Jumping Mouse for the rest of the night.

"Amazing."

"Good night Red."

19

Red Hot Green Mountains

 By the time Red Hot and I had hiked two weeks together, it was clear to me that he was a special person. When you hike 8 to 10 hours a day together, camp together, eat together and struggle together, you get to know each other. It wasn't long before I dropped the formalities and called him by his first name, Red. Red Hot's real name is Rob. As is customary, he earned his trail name within the first few weeks on the trail.

Unlike me, Red began planning his hike years earlier. Over the last year he saved, bought gear, researched the trail and dehydrated 180 meals. Self-employed, he put his job on hold to chase his life-long dream. He even sold his truck. His support crew consisted of his wife of 30 years and two grown daughters who drove him to Georgia. Renee, his wife, was charting his progress from home with her own guidebook. She even met him on the trail and hiked the entire state of New Jersey with him! At home in Western Maine, his Mom and Dad kept a long narrow map of the trail on the wall, and marked his position with a pushpin every morning. If you asked him, he'd tell you that being away from all of them was the hardest part of the hike.

One day at the beginning of his thru-hike and while camped with a group of hikers, Rob offered another hiker some Red Hot sauce for her food. The group was amazed when he broke out a container of Red Hot hot sauce that he had dehydrated in preparation for his trip. They passed it around and dubbed him "Red Hot."

Red and I were close to the same age, grew up playing outdoors, had a love for the woods and water, and lived in New England. We had lots to talk about. His Maine accent added credibility to his stories, of which he had many. The miles flew by when we got to talking and telling stories; before we knew it, it would be time to stop and camp. We both liked to stealth camp, so he would find a space, big enough to set his tent, and I would use nearby trees. This system worked well.

As a NoBo (North Bounder), hitting Vermont gave me a new sense of excitement. There was less than 600 miles remaining, the area was familiar, I was back in peak form and I was still flying high from seeing my close friends in southern New England. I couldn't wait to climb all the fire towers that I knew were ahead, and the next big challenge: The White Mountains of New Hampshire. Red was feeling it, too. Every step he took was bringing him closer to Maine, his home state.

Boulders of Bennington

The trail on the south side of Rte. 9 near Bennington, Vermont, is amazing. The dramatic staircase has been constructed out of boulders that makes you happy you are traveling north, not south. The sheer steepness, and the scope of the construction project that was needed to create it, are astounding. Concentration while descending this quarter mile is a necessity. About halfway down, I lost my concentration on the wet rocks, slipped and fell. I couldn't just pop back up and continue. I left the trail and tumbled like a rolling stone 20 feet below. I could hear Red Hot asking me if I was okay, but I wasn't sure myself. I told him to "give me a minute" while I caught my breath and assessed myself. The first contact I made with the ground was on top of my pack which knocked the wind out of me. It saved me from the stone step that I initially landed on when my feet slipped forward. I was covered with mud and took a few lumps on my arms, but seemed okay. When I came to a stop, I had been rolling like a barrel and landed facing up the hill towards Red. The only thing stopping me from rolling another 20 feet, were two little saplings about two inches in diameter.

I felt a sharp pain in my lower abdomen when I attempted to get up, so I removed my pack and crawled back up to the trail. I rolled the pack a few feet, crawled up to it, and then, rolled it again. When it was close enough to grab, Red pulled it up, then helped me up. We looked at those little saplings and realized how lucky I was that they were there – the other 20 feet was worse. I reminded myself that sometimes I need a little bad luck to remind me how lucky I am.

I made it to the bottom without any more mishaps, but just in case, Red Hot was nearby. When we arrived at the trailhead on Rte. 9, Mrs. IceMan, a familiar face, was waiting for IceMan. IceMan was attempting a supported thru-hike. Mrs. IceMan picked him up each night, at a trailhead, and returned him each morning. Together they were working their way to Katahdin, one motel at a time. He is a healthy man, in his seventies, with a strong New Jersey accent. He knocked himself out on a low hanging tree and fell off a bog bridge along the way, but he is tough. He almost quit when he was stuck waist deep in mud for 45 minutes, but continued on. He was on track to finish when I last saw him in Maine.

Mrs. IceMan gave me a few bottles of water to wash the mud off, and I checked for injuries. I had a few abrasions and a sore abdomen, but I would be fine. It was late afternoon and I decided to go into Bennington to visit the Bennington Monument, a revolutionary war monument, for my videos. I was also due to post the latest episode. Everyone had footage of the trail, I was trying to find interesting off-trail content to add. IceMan gave me a ride into town, which was about five miles away.

Red Hot remained on the trail and we planned to meet up the following evening. I agreed to hike late the next day until I found his camp, and he agreed to leave me a sign so I wouldn't pass him in the dark.

I left my pack in a hotel room while I walked through the town to the monument. It is a limestone obelisk, around 300 feet, with an ele-vator inside so visitors can ride up to the observation level. I could see it from town but it took me an additional hour to actually reach it. It was closed, of course, so I snapped a few pictures and turned around and headed back to the hotel. The monument was high atop a hill and was the last thing the sun hit before falling behind the surrounding mountains. It was beautiful, and I was happy I went.

This night turned into a marathon. I was up until 2 a.m., sitting in the lobby and posting my latest video. The Wi-Fi wasn't working in my room and the public computer in the lobby was very slow. The concierge kept an eye on my things while it loaded, and I went to the Food Lion. I bought some American chop suey, potato salad and a gallon of sweet tea. It was wonderful.

The secret to getting back to the trail from a motel is to go to the free continental breakfast. I would walk in with my backpack, smile at everyone and toss out a bunch of "good morning" greetings. For the most part, most of the travelers aren't hiking; they are on an adventure or journey of their own. These friendly travelers will soon begin with their questions, and when they learn you need a ride back to the trail... they offer. It is the ultimate "yogi" challenge.

When I got to the free breakfast that morning, no "yogi-ing" was needed. Shark Bait was there with his Mom. She drove out from eastern Massachusetts to spend the day with him. She drove me to the trail, complete with a hug. *The trail will provide.* They dropped me off by 8 am, and I fell in line with the other hikers like ants on a log. The trail was easy, the weather was great and I was packing a day's worth of sweet tea. Since I began hiking with Red Hot, I hadn't used my iPod; we just talked all day. I stuck my earbud(s) in and set out to catch him.

My lower abdomen was causing me discomfort throughout the day, so I took my time. I started looking for Red's sign when the sun began to fade. He said I'd see it. I saw it... from about a quarter of a mile away. The woods were dark and I hadn't turned my headlight on yet, so it was easy to see. Red Hot built a campfire – or more aptly, a signal fire. The orange glow lit a perfect circle of light and when I got close, I made out the silhouette of Red watching over it. With his hand on a seven-foot poking pole, he looked like an Appalachian Trail Wizard.

When I reached his campsite I found his red neckerchief tied to a branch, hanging like a flag. The campsite was about 30 yards off the trail and had a big circle of rocks for campfires. The open space was well-used and clear of debris, and thanks to Red's blaze, no mosquitoes. As I handed his bandana back to him, I asked if the flag was overkill, he just said, "Hey, I'm an Eagle Scout, no such thing."

We sat on the ground leaning against a couple trees and enjoyed the fire. Every few minutes Red would add a log or poke the flames, until it eventually burned down to coals. He then double-checked the ashes, raking and spreading them, until he was certain they met all Eagle Scout regulations. Then we turned in.

"Good night Red"

"Goodnight Sam I Am"

It was the last thing we said every night until we reached Katahdin.

Vermont quickly moved its way up to my favorite state thus far. The trail worked its way through the Green Mountains, offering dark cool forests, silent chairlift-topped summits and tall fire towers. I climbed almost every fire tower on the trail. Even the ones with locked hatches were high enough to offer a view from above the trees. The views never failed to take my breath away. Modern technology had replaced their usefulness and many have already been disassembled; the concrete footings left as reminders, dot the trail. I would climb the narrow steps to the top – to a view that I fear won't be accessible much longer. Red Hot fought his fear of heights and climbed to the top, snapped a picture or two, and promptly returned to the safety of solid ground.

Slowly, Red was beginning to leave his comfort zone. Until we started hiking together he hadn't climbed a tower, and he rarely left the trail unless it was for a few hours to wash clothes, grab a shower and resupply. Like the fire towers, he started to join me when I left the trail in search of "additional content." That was the term we used. It meant getting everything we could from our hike. That content might mean blue blazing – following a side trail to a waterfall or viewpoint – or taking a road walk to a diner or a trip to a landmark like the Bennington Monument.

We found some additional content in Manchester, Vermont. We were closing in on Red's home turf and Mrs. Red Hot came out to spend the day with her husband. She picked us up at the trailhead in the morning and offered to take us wherever we wanted. Naturally, we went to a "breakfast restaurant." Manchester Center Vermont is kind of a yuppie town; they don't call them diners there. It was nice to finally meet her. After hiking with Red for 150 miles and sharing stories from home, I felt like I knew her already.

We took care of some hygiene and laundry at the local hostel, and then set out to explore the town. If you visit the Green Mountain House Hiker Hostel, you will see Red's worn boots hanging from the porch, he left them with about a hundred other pair that are retired there.

Having the luxury of a driver and four wheels, Red and I weren't limited to the main streets and hiker-friendly routes to travel, so we ventured out of town a little. We decided to go to a museum – The American Museum of Fly Fishing, to be specific. Our mutual love of all finned creatures and the techniques by which they are captured made this museum a must-see. You can imagine our disappointment when we found the doors locked.

Similar to the Woodland Jumping Mouse situation, we had to resort to innovative thinking, so I knocked. I stood on the granite steps and knocked long and loud. Of course, I wasn't surprised when no one answered, so we turned and headed down the steps toward the parking lot. That's when the door opened! A man stuck his head out and asked if he could help us! We introduced ourselves and asked if we could go in.

It took some serious trout-talk and a little begging, but we were allowed to go in and self-tour the entire collection of historical gear, pictures, displays and literature. We were thrilled. Our decision to hike had eliminated our spring and summer fishing, and this side trip helped to fill the void. After our visit, we went directly to the Orvis Flagship Store, the Macy's of outdoor stores.

Eventually, our day off was winding down, so Mrs. Red Hot drove us back to the trail, where we did some tailgating before heading back into the woods. Red cooked burgers and hot dogs on a small gas grill, and a few lucky hikers were treated to some trail magic. Before Mrs. Red Hot left, we toasted our beer cans to another great day, and tossed the empties in the car (Leave No Trace). As we waived our goodbyes, Red yelled "We're IN THE ZONE BABY!" He used this expression whenever things were going exceptionally good.

China Rock, who wasn't feeling "the zone," came out of the woods with a deep gash on her knee just before we left Mrs. Red Hot. She had taken a nasty fall and landed hard. Within minutes, Mrs. Red Hot had her in the car and heading towards town for treatment. *The trail will provide...*

Hiking with Red made the days easier, but the Green Mountains were increasing in elevation requiring more work on our part. When we climbed Killington it was the first 4,000 foot mountain since Virginia. The trail doesn't actually go to the peak, so Red and I decided to take the side trail up. The narrow path was steep and treacherous, surrounded by stunted mountain bushes. By the time we summited, our clothes were wet with sweat despite the cool temperature and stiff winds. After hiking all afternoon to get there, I was shocked to find people with flip flops, little kids and the smell of perfume, dryer sheets and shampoo blowing in the wind. It looked like a Patagonia convention had just let out!

Killington Peak is home to New England's largest ski area. The mountaintop lodge is open year round for skiers, leaf peepers and special functions. The people with the Patagonia's and flip flops rode the gondola from the base where there was a music festival going on. I talked Red into going a little further off-trail in search for real food. We went into the lodge and I bought a burger, fries and a coke. Total: $16.00.

The view was worth the hike. Standing on the peak offered impressive views of the neighboring mountains, deep valleys and radio towers. There was a fire tower there, too, but it was off limits. Red and I fist-bumped as he said, "Another one down!" That would become another routine we repeated at the top of each mountain.

We returned to the AT via the same steep and narrow trail that got us to the peak. Our mountaintop experience wasn't nearly as moving or peaceful as we'd become used to, and it was good to be back in the woods. We camped a few hundred feet down the mountain where the nighttime temps dipped into the 40s. Fall was coming.

Red told me about a tick bite he discovered while hiking in New Jersey. It bit him on the thigh and displayed the telltale red bulls-eye. This wasn't the first time he had been infected by the tick-borne illness, so he was familiar with the symptoms. He hoped he'd be able to finish his hike before he began to get sick, but no such luck.

He called his wife, who then called his doctor, and just like that, there was a prescription waiting for him in Rutland. Next stop... Rutland, Vermont.

I introduced Red to another first: hitch-hiking. Up to this point, he was able to commute back and fourth from the trail from helpful Trail Angels and paid shuttle drivers. The trip to the Hannaford Supermarket was almost ten miles away, and they had his prescription for antibiotics. Hannaford is a large supermarket chain in the northeast. Locals pronounce it, "Hanafids."

Red was a little more cautious than I was, and hitching was out of his comfort zone. I assured him that we'd be okay, and eventually, he reluctantly stuck his thumb out. We positioned ourselves in a good area allowing prospective rides plenty of room to pull over, removed our packs and started thumbing. We watched about 50 cars approach from the long hill and zoom past without a glance.

I checked on Red, who was behind me, and I could see he wasn't putting his heart into it. I gave him the finer points of hitching, like a big smile, enthusiastic thumb presentation and waving to the cars traveling in the opposite direction (in case they come back before we catch a ride). He did his best, to no avail; no one was stopping.

I removed my bandana, because Red actually told me that I looked "kinda scary," and that he wouldn't pick me up either. Then he tried to convince me to wear my bandana as a neckerchief, in the spirit of the 40 million Scout members around the world. He said it looked friendlier. I conceded, and wouldn't you know it, the very next vehicle stopped and picked us up! The little Ford Ranger was loaded down, and we crammed into the cab. Vermont's newest Trail Angel drove us all the way to Hanafids.

We decided to turn the town stop into a NERO, or near-zero-mile day, and rented a room. We went out twice for McDonald's and Wendy's. Other than that, we enjoyed the air conditioning and watched a North Woods Law marathon on TV. The game warden TV show, filmed in Maine, was a favorite of both of us. There are five New England teams: Patriots, Bruins, Red Sox, Celtics... and North Woods

Law. In the morning, we took public transportation back to the trail which made Red feel better; he didn't have to hitch.

I broke my glasses and had been hiking for a few days without them. Everything was a blur. Thankfully, I had a spare on standby in Connecticut, and I had to take a side trip to a post office a few miles off-trail to get them. Red was suffering from a lack of energy and headaches the last few days from his Lyme medication, so he stayed on-trail while I went into Woodstock, Vermont. I planned to find him when he camped, like we did before.

Woodstock's post office is located in the general store. The town looked like something Norman Rockwell would paint. I hitched the short ride down the rural road, past old homes, freshly mown lawns and a narrow bridge. The general store is located on a sweeping bend in the road, opposite a small dirt parking area with two picnic tables. Judging from the colorful puddles of melted cream, people sit there to eat ice cream next to the small brook that ran past. There is a ski area just up the road a piece, but as far as I could tell, this was the center of town.

When I stepped into the store I was greeted with delicious aromas of the daily specials, and the antique building had air conditioning. The postmaster found my parcel, and I was thrilled to be able to see again. The first thing I read was the menu handwritten on a small chalkboard and I ordered a large meatball grinder. (They don't sell subs in New England.) The wooden floor creaked and cracked as I browsed around the store. There were unique items to buy as well as antiques displayed throughout. I tried to identify them while I waited for my order.

I took my grinder, along with some chips and Dr. Pepper, past the old gas pumps to the picnic tables. Trout and Hercules, a couple young bucks in their early twenties, were sitting in the shade catching up with the world news. They had a stack of newspapers and passed them back and forth as they finished reading each section. Red and I would get passed by them multiple times before Maine. They hiked like hell, slept late and then passed us again. We always knew when they were coming: Hercules' music would be cranking and we could hear their conversations point-1 away.

(As a side note: They were two smart, fun guys. Red and I enjoyed hearing them hiking through the woods. In Lyme Center, New Hampshire, Red and I found their phones plugged in on the porch of Dr. Bill Ackerly, a trail legend, and we took a bunch of selfies. We never saw them there, so we enjoyed an ice cream, signed "The Ice Cream Man's" guest book and moved on. When they passed us later, no mention of the pictures was made.)

I got back to the trail two hours after I left, which put Red Hot four to five miles ahead. A strong thunderstorm came through, however, and set me back further. I was never in a rush. After hiking in a few thunderstorms and getting soaked, I usually decided to wait them out. When I felt one coming, I'd set up my tarp low to the ground and climb under. Thunderstorms usually blow by within a half hour, some longer; you never know until you are in it. It only takes a few minutes to get soaked for the rest of the day, so I avoided it by taking a nap. Like noise, silence wakes me as well. When the relaxing sound of rain on my tarp stops, I wake up and resume hiking. On my luckier days, it would rain for two hours. On the days it rained all day, I just embraced it and hiked.

It was dark when I found Red's neckerchief hanging from a branch. I shined my light up and down the hillside, but couldn't see his tent. When I called out to him, his tent lit up much higher than I expected and he yelled, "I picked out a couple trees up here for you!" He couldn't find a suitable pair lower down on the hill, and he didn't want me to stumble around looking in the dark.

When we left camp in the morning, we estimated that we'd cross into New Hampshire by midafternoon. We hiked with the familiar excitement that always comes before a state line. We were aware of the daunting White Mountains, and knew we were approaching, quite possibly, the most challenging stretch of the trail thus far. Before we got there, however, Vermont had a few surprises up her sleeve.

The trail had led us through beautiful pine forests, around cool lakes, over high mountains and along long bog bridges, which were no more than a thick board supported by logs on either end. Sometimes the bog bridges would wind through the forest for long stretches; others were a single plank. The simple plank walkways protected the soil from turning to mud with the heavy traffic, and allowed the roots to remain covered by the rich soil. I thought the ATC should do that in Pennsylvania. It would make navigating the rocks easier!

As we were passing through one of the many mountaintop meadows, we noticed black raspberries. There was about an acre of them. Red and I love wild berries, and without a word, we dropped our packs and began eating. With our heads down, we grazed through the prickers like a couple foraging bears only looking forward enough to find the next heavy cluster of ripe berries.

After about 45 minutes, we ate our way back to our packs with blue tongues and stained hands, lifted our packs and hiked off. Happy and full, we accepted our bloody thorn-scratched legs as a badge of courage and a fair price to pay for the sweet plump berries.

When we came out of the woods, the trail led us down the mountain on a rural paved road crossing the White River in Hartford, Vermont. It's a modern bridge, made of concrete with steel rails. It looked brand new. As we crossed it, enjoying the view of the river, we heard a loud bell ringing. Red immediately got excited because, during his research, he learned about this AT tradition.

We crossed the bridge which landed us at the door of Linda and Randy. Linda was the bell ringer. They invited us into their home, fed us pancakes and hot coffee, and told us some of their Appalachian Trail stories. In 2002, their nephew hiked the trail and came home with tales of Trail Angels and the kindness he received. Since then, Linda and Randy have fed thousands of hikers, calling them in from the bridge with the unmistakable ringing of the bell.

Before breakfast, I walked back out to the bridge and jumped off. Standing on the railing, I executed a front flip to the water 30 feet below. I felt like a teenager! Back at the house, Trout from West Virginia, Mainer from, well... Maine, and Red Hot, teased me about acting my age. They rated my dive at an 8.5.

9.3 miles separated us from the Connecticut River, the border between Vermont and New Hampshire (pronounced "Hampsha"), but with a belly full of pancakes, berries and coffee, we had plenty of energy. Other than an occasional stop to drink cold mountain water, we hiked like we were running late for work.

The last mile or so, the trail was filled with obstacles. The bridge crossing into New Hampshire was reached by a long road walk. The white blazes that led us through the mountains were now painted on telephone poles. We walked through a quiet neighborhood, sparsely traveled, with modest homes. Both sides of the street were lined with coolers, plastic bins, garbage bags and gallons of water. We had hit Trail Magic Heaven!

Inside the coolers we found cold soda and water. Tupperware containers were filled with fresh baked banana bread, cookies and candy.

The plastic bins had trail bars and hiker supplies, and there were bags for our trash. Red and I were astonished! It was midafternoon and everyone must be at work, because other than a middle-of-the-road visit with Warm-and-Toasty from Florida, the neighborhood was a ghost town. If it wasn't for the friendly hand-written notes from the mysterious Trail Angels, it would have been a test of my morals. It doesn't feel right taking something without saying thank you. It felt like I was stealing!

Red and I drank a coke, ate a piece of banana bread and left a thank you note before exploring every cooler and box on the street. You never know when you might find a lobster; after all, we were in New England.

We didn't find a lobster, but we were definitely in the Zone. Red and I crossed into New Hampshire, the 13th State, with more energy, excitement and enthusiasm than we had felt up to this point. His positive attitude, sense of humor and willingness to look for added content (like frequent diner runs), had improved my hiking enjoyment exponentially. We were determined to make it to Katahdin together.

20

New Hampshire

 The first SoBo (South Bounder) I met was in Massachusetts, when my friend Pauly did trail magic in North Adams. Since that day, Red and I hadn't met one we liked. It wasn't because they were rude or mean. They weren't snobby – most were just the opposite. Most were on their way home to the east coast's southern states, doing what Red and I were doing... walking home. The reason we didn't like them is because they never had anything good to say.

For the last 150 miles, every SoBo we met was carrying news of awful trails, painful climbs and deep mud. "Wait until you get to Vermont, the trails are so muddy." Or "Wait until you hit the Whites, they are brutal." "The bugs are awful." No matter how nice we were, or how nice they were, they always snuck some warning of what was to come.

Every time Red and I passed these bearers of negativity, we would say (to each other), "Have a nice Thanksgiving in the Smokies... know it all." We became creative with our post-SoBo comments: "You, 1,800

miles to go, us, 400. We'll be done by the time you hit New Jersey!"
"You still smell like REI. Talk to us when you reach Harpers Ferry."

It became maddening. We would meet them, stop for some friendly
conversation, and then they would hit us with some unfavorable trail
report. "You better be ready for Mt. Washington." I thought I'd have
to hold Red back. Who were they to talk to us like that? Didn't they
know we had already hiked 80% of the way?

Red told me that the first SoBo that didn't do that was getting a
kiss. We'd have to see. A couple times it was close, but on saying good-
bye, it always slipped out. "You better get out your cold weather gear,
it's cold up north." We would throw our hands up with an outburst
and the SoBo had no idea what we were doing. We swore not to do
that to any SoBo – no matter how much they tried to shake us up.

Dartmouth

Hanover is the first town we hit in New Hampshire; it's the home of
Dartmouth College. The Dartmouth Common is a beautifully maintained field/lawn surrounded by big shade trees. We were swallowed
up with the activity and moved seemingly unnoticed, while walking
through the Frisbee throwers, blanket sleepers, young lovers and giant
chess, chess players. We were still in the zone judging by the large
farmer's market with tents brimming with people shopping for honey,
fresh veggies and natural soap.

Big collegiate-looking buildings surrounded the once well-used
pasture, then athletic fields and now recreation center. Public transportation and common traffic drove around the perimeter, but due
to the massive space and except for the occasional honk, only those
close to the edges could hear them. A group of hikers lounged in the
grass, enjoying the relaxing mood and Ivy League setting. As for Red

and I, we could smell the Jamaican food coming from the temporary marketplace and wasted no time searching it out.

We dodged the mountain bikers and baby strollers, passed up on samples of gluten-free bakery treats and canned bacon products, and took our place in line at the most popular tent on the Common. The hard-working servers piled their traditional food on our flimsy paper plates with a half-comedy, half-concession flair. We gladly paid the man for the spicy dish and found a bench in the shade to eat. When we finished our meal we went into one of the dorms, found a lavatory and washed the spices off our hands before we accidentally rubbed our eyes.

When our hands were no longer a threat to our health, we headed through the town, stopped for a cold beer and slice of pizza, and then camped in the woods behind the athletic field. From here on in, when people asked Red and I how we met, we always answered by saying, "We went to Dartmouth together." If they pressed it, we would come clean, but if not, we left it alone. (It never hurts to let people think you are smart.)

We packed up early and went to a fancy breakfast place where they gave free crullers to passing hikers. The coffee was great, our meal was filling and the cruller was yummy. We paid our bill which wasn't cheap, but worth it, and then we left town before a PETA rally broke out or something.

Our enthusiasm for reaching New Hampshire remained high, and we managed to hike about 17 miles from Hanover despite our diner-delay. We were looking for a place to camp at the top of a long climb when Red heard the distinctive call of a peregrine falcon. Following his lead, I followed him as he turned off the trail onto a smaller trail with hopes of getting a glance at the fastest animal in the world.

Over the miles, I learned to trust trails. We trusted this one and we couldn't believe our luck. The trees opened up to a spectacular view, and standing on the top of the cliffs, was the falcon calling out to the valley. We watched the stunning bird of prey as he seemed to pose for us. We took some pictures, but not wanting to disturb him, or her, they were taken from too much of a distance. Like most pictures of nature, these would pale in comparison to the real thing.

We backed out and resisted the urge to camp on the cliffs. We decided to camp close though, and take a peek in the morning. If the falcon is away, we might check out the cliffs. We broke up to find a good spot in the woods like two guys looking for a lost dog.

I stumbled onto a trail and called to Red. He had become accustomed to following my exploring behaviors. It led us out of the woods, through a small grass and weeded meadow. Beyond the meadow we arrived at the top of a ski area – complete with a ski patrol building and a chairlift. Red did some research on his phone and trail guide, and deduced that we were at the top of the Dartmouth Skyway, the college-owned ski area.

It was an unlikely place to camp, but he set his tent and I used my poles to erect my tarp into a tent-like shelter, and we camped on the summit. It was a cool night, much different to the heat of the day, and I was only moderately pestered by the insects as I slept on the ground under my tarp. Thousands of skiers had swooshed over this very spot for years. On this night, however, it was deserted except for Red and I. The clear sky and bright stars never seemed to engulf us in darkness, and we could see the hulking silhouette of the chairlifts and unloading station throughout the night. They served as a reminder that we were trespassers.

We left at daybreak fearing we might be discovered, and returned to the cliff that Red learned was named Holts Ledge. The falcon was gone so we ventured past the dilapidated chain-link fence to take in the view to the east. It was spectacular. The valleys were cloud-filled as far as we could see, looking like a white ocean. Once again, photos would do it no justice.

Now, I'm not an overly religious man. I trust my relationship with my creator and live my life in a way, I believe, is pleasing to Him. As I hiked my way north and witnessed the incredible unceasing evidence of a greater power, I was continually humbled by my smallness. I won't get too spiritual with you, but mornings like these leave no doubt in my mind that there is something, or someone, out there. (I just hope we aren't in a petri dish in a lab somewhere.)

We got our first taste of the White Mountains when we hiked over. We were fresh and well fed before tackling the first of the skyscrapers that New Hampshire is famous for. Red's family met us and we all spent the night at a campground where we car-camped. Renee, Mrs. Red Hot, spent the day conducting trail magic with their experienced Trail Angel daughters Lily and Ali. After sitting around the campfire and eating all night, we were delivered back to the trail in the morning. We headed up the first 4,000 foot mountain in the "Whites" with our new hiking companion, Ali.

She insisted on carrying her own pack while she hiked the roughly nine mile portion of the AT with her Dad and me. The weather started out rainy, but cleared after a thorough soaking. We considered this our welcome to the Whites and as promised, it was a tough hike. Red and I hiked on with our normal trail antics. Ali followed close behind trying to wrap her head around our mindless conversations and silly singing. During a rest stop, Ali told us that we must be spending too much time together because when we sang, she couldn't tell when I stopped and her Dad picked up!

When we popped out of the woods and above tree-line, we realized that on this rare occasion we were following the line of cairns by ourselves. The summit, too, was ours alone. We marveled at the 4,800-foot view. To the east we could see Franconia Ridge, our next destination. To the west lay the Green Mountains of Vermont and the Adirondacks of New York. The sky had cleared and the 360-degree view was stunning.

We hiked together for a while on the way down, but I eventually went ahead so Red could spend some one-on-one time with Ali. When I started in Georgia, the rocks were small and easy to navigate; up here in New Hampshire, they had grown in size. They don't call it The Granite State for nothing. I was from The Nutmeg State. (Talk about emasculating!)

Before I went ahead, we took a rest on the rocks in the middle of the trail. We ended up sitting there for quite a while telling stories, and laughing until we cried. It is one of those trail moments I will remember forever. Like I said before, there are some special moments that really stand out... that was one of them.

The last few miles I hiked alone. I was high on life and happy to see Red enjoying his time with Ali. If I wasn't careful, I could easily become sad. They reminded me of the fun I would be having with my boys, if they were here. I missed them dearly.

There was no time to be sad. The trail following the Beaver Brook Cascades is treacherous! There are a few places on the trail that can be fatal, this is one. Much of the trail is exposed rock with metal rungs to grab and wooden steps anchored for footing. The earlier rain added a little extra challenge making the wood steps "slicker than snot on a glass doorknob!" It's not impossible though. I was told that the deaths that occur on that mountain usually come from hypothermia not falls. (How reassuring.)

I met Renee at the trail parking lot, where she gave trail magic to hikers all afternoon while waiting for us. By now, we were familiar with most of the NoBos within a week of us (each direction), and when she told the hikers she was Red Hot's wife, they embraced her as family. Simple Man, Chocolate, Dash, Turbo, Tigger and Mud Magnet stopped as well as China Rock. Red and I hadn't seen her since southern Vermont when she hurt her knee.

Red and Ali came out of the woods just before dark. We had a barbecue, said our good-byes and waived to them as they drove off. Red, who is a happy guy, was exceptionally happy as we headed into the woods to find a place to camp. It had been a great 24 hours.

By the time we had reached Lincoln, New Hampshire, not exactly on the trail, I was dealing with two specific problems: the stitch in my lower abdomen turned out to be a hernia and I had a severe case of poison ivy. I was dealing with the hernia by stopping a few times a day and pushing it back in. (I know... too much information.) I didn't want to seek medical attention because I had a hunch I would be advised to stop hiking, so I decided to go as far as I could. When it got too painful, I would ask Red to stop for a minute, push it back in, catch my breath, and continue hiking. It sounded like a croaking frog when I did that, and it was a seven on the medical pain chart, but after a minute, I felt much better. It really grossed Red out though.

The poison ivy was much more of a nuisance. Somewhere, I walked through poison ivy and my ankles were badly affected. I was miserable. It hurt to hike, and then it would itch at night. I had no ointment so I tried to ride it out. Unfortunately, it kept getting worse; I was losing my mind! The night Red and I camped at the Dartmouth ski area I was desperate for relief. My ankles were red and swollen, and the itching was making me insane. In a moment of agony, I made the foolhardy decision to spray them with 100% DEET. About a minute later my hernia was the least of my worries! Eventually the burning subsided and I thought I found the cure for poison ivy. I remember telling Red, who tried his best to talk me out of the bad idea, that he was worried about nothing.

By morning my poison ivy became blistered, resembling burns. Within two days the huge blisters filled with fluid and popped, which immediately became infected. When I peeled my socks off at the end of the day, they stuck to my ankles. (I know... Red was grossed out, too.)

We hitched a ride from Walking Home, a friendly hiker from Maine, whose wife was visiting him in Lincoln. He drove to the trail and brought us into town where we rented a room; I'd seek out treatment while we were there. With the help of Google, I found a medical center.

After breakfast Red and I split up. I walked to the doctor's office in the pouring rain only to find a sign taped to the door: "This is a private practice. NO WALK INS. Established patients ONLY."

I looked at my reflection in the glass door and saw a wet, bearded, homeless-looking man. I decided to try anyway. If my infection got any worse it would end my hike. I went in. I tried to shake the water off my raincoat in the entrance, then walked into the lobby. The two receptionists looked down as I approached, each looking like they were hoping I'd go to the other. I greeted them with an enthusiastic "Good Morning!" I even said hi to another patient who was seated in the waiting area. I was unignorably friendly.

I pulled the same maneuver Don Knotts pulled on me in the shelter: I approached the first receptionist to look up. I had a feeling I wasn't the first hiker to seek help, judging from the sign, so I would have to plead my case before she turned me away. "I saw the sign on the door, and I wouldn't have come in if it wasn't urgent." I didn't stop, "I have a severe case of poison ivy that has become infected and I need medical attention." Before she cut me off, I finished with "AND... I have insurance. "

The puddle I was making by the desk was getting big, and my beard dripped while I spoke, but I gave her my best smile while raising my Blue Cross card and license so she could see them. She still hadn't spoken, yet, she just looked over at the other woman. I thought they would team up and tell me all their policies and how they wished they could help, but the second lady said, "I can get you in at 11:20, if you can wait." It was 11:00 and as promised, I was in an examination room twenty minutes later peeling off my socks.

"Well, it's not the worst case I've ever seen, but it's pretty bad." I was glad he saw the urgency. "We'll give you a shot and a 'script and you'll be on your way." A half an hour later I was back out in the rain walking to the pharmacy. Twenty years working in the prison was no picnic, but all those roll calls and missed holidays were paying off. The power of medical benefits is understated.

We woke to sunny skies the next morning, and to our delight, we had breakfast with some hikers we hadn't seen in a while. We sat together in the dining room of the motel destroying the continental breakfast. We listened to Walking Home as he outlined his plan to "get through" the rest of the hike. Summiting Katahdin was taking over everyone's thoughts as we closed in on Maine.

Mrs. Walking Home took us back to the trail in waves and we headed up the most dramatic section of the Whites, Franconia Ridge. We left the Notch on wet trails but under dry skies, and headed up, up, up. The terminology was changing as we hiked north: gaps were now notches; shelters were now lean-tos; and there were mountain accommodations called huts. For about 150 bucks, you can reserve a bunk in a hut, have an awesome meal, fresh water and clean bathrooms. They are located throughout the Whites and primarily used by vacationers who want to hike in the mountains without giving up all the comforts of home. The staff tend to be college students and they are great hosts. Part of their job is to hike in all the food and supplies for the guests as well as hike out all the garbage.

Hiking in New Hampshire gets a little more complicated. It is a managed by a very old mountain club and they are steeped in tradition. Like most of the AT, the trails in that state were established long before Benton MacKaye ever dreamed of one long trail from Georgia to Maine. Part of the tradition relies on navigating specific trails by name and less use of the white blazes I had become so dependent on. The result was that Red and I got lost... more than once.

We were expected to navigate areas with dramatic and cool names like Kinsman Ridge, Franconia Ridge, Crawford Pass, Thunderstorm Jct., The Presidential Range, Wildcat Ridge, the list goes on. In the words of Gator from New Hampshire, "It's a new level of pain." I promised I wouldn't go "trail guide" on you, but with all these different sections came some of the most dramatic, physically demanding and weather-exposed hiking on the trail so far. The high peaks and above tree-line terrain was both grueling and jaw-dropping. It was my new favorite state.

Red and I had no desire to merely "get through" the White Mountains; we were savoring each mountaintop and viewpoint like tourists in a strange land. The remote trails led to astonishing views before dropping back into the alpine forest. If one state had to be voted "Captain of the Trail" based on pristine beauty and its rugged presence, it would be New Hampshire.

The Zealand Falls Hut is one of the many huts located in the White Mountains. Although geared for the backpackers who want a roof over their head and a hot meal, the Hut staff is welcoming to long-distance hikers, offering clean water and leftovers. At 150 bucks a night, most long-distance backpackers opt to camp elsewhere. For a few lucky ones, however, they open their doors. "Work for stay" is a common practice where the hut manager exchanges lodging and a meal in trade for chores rendered by the hiker. The lodging consists of sleeping on the floor of the dining area, but the food is all you can eat.

Red and I arrived at the Zealand Falls Hut around 4:30 p.m. We weren't actively looking for work for stay; we were happy with our normal camping routine. Due to the timing, however, hut managers don't offer the deal until late afternoon, we inquired anyway. Eliza, Tidbit and Roger, the "croo" there, agreed with one condition: we conduct a presentation to the guests about thru-hiking. We weren't thru-hikers yet, but it was Mexican fare. We'd wing it.

We didn't know what to expect, so Red and I decided to formulate a plan. Our plan was to try and meet as many people as we could beforehand, get a feel for the room and tailor the presentation to them. Mostly though, we hoped that if they were already acquainted with us, they wouldn't boo us off the stage.

When the evening meal was finished and the guests were assembled, we were called into the dining area. The group was 35 strong and represented the local states like Massachusetts and Rhode Island as well as some from as far away as Oregon and Minnesota. Chachi and Jasapher were from Chicago and earned their trail names recently. It was a diverse and energetic group, ranging from pre-teen to pre-seventies, and they welcomed Red and I like we were friends.

Two hours went by as we answered their questions and they listened to our stories. It didn't seem like they were disappointed that most of them had more hiking experience then Red and I; in fact, it was quite the opposite. Our "regular guy" or "non-expert" point of view was relatable. Narrating some of our adventures got laughs, others gasps, but not one beautifully smelling person left until Tidbit took his dining area back. "Let's give Sam I Am and Red Hot a hand!"

We mingled with the guests for the next hour, enjoying our new friends and honestly, I felt like a rock star (literally). Someone saw a shooting star and the whole group went outside. We watched the meteor shower in awe as the long bright streaks entertained us every few minutes. One by one, the trail-weary guests retired to their bunks and only Red and I remained on the front porch.

We were still pretty wired from our impromptu presentation – and very relieved we weren't thrown out. Even though sleeping indoors had been part of our deal, we decided to sleep outside. The meteors continued and despite the cold night, we weren't going to miss the show. It was 3 a.m. before I decided to close my eyes for good; Red had been snoring since 1.

Mount Washington is over 6,200 feet above sea level and is the second highest point on the trail. Red and I felt like we had been drinking from the fountain of youth with our lean strong bodies, and we looked forward to anything the trail put in front of us. The last time we climbed this high we were in the Smokies – and it wasn't as fun. To get to the summit of "The Big W," we had to ascend a rigorous 12-mile climb.

The climb itself held all the beauty, challenge and thrills that the rest of New Hampshire held with a noticeable difference – lots and lots of people. We had become accustomed to the crowded trails in the White Mountains National Forest; after all, it is located within a day's drive from Boston, New York, Hartford, Connecticut, Providence, Rhode Island, and Portland, Maine. The ability to step out of your car and disappear into the wilderness is a big draw up there.

The last mile and a half of the climb was virtually like walking in a line. The fragile alpine vegetation to the sides of the trail was off limits, so Red and I fell in with the weekenders who ventured out with their colorful, sweet smelling hiking clothes dotting the way. Parents were coaxing their tired children, and children were coaxing their tired parents. Frustrated health-nuts were jogging in place waiting for downhill traffic to pass (etiquette calls for uphill traffic to pass), and whole families stopped, blocking the trail. Meanwhile, we watched the clouds begin to enshroud the summit weather station and cell towers, while we slowly crept toward them. We didn't consider ourselves "trail snobs" but we realized we had become a little spoiled. We patiently put our egos in check.

Our summit on August 15th coincided with the annual Mt. Washington Bicycle Hill Climb. Due to the dense fog and direction of approach, we weren't aware of this event until we arrived on top of the mountain. To our surprise, there were thousands of people in attendance! There were people driving up the mountain, riding bikes and riding the Cog Railroad! The cafeteria-style restaurant reminded me of a modern ski lodge: crowded to capacity, loud and disappointing.

Red got in line with 40 spandex-clad cyclists, most holding their bikes, for a picture near the summit sign. I waited back and took a picture of him getting his picture taken. We couldn't get off that mountain fast enough! It wasn't what we were hoping for, but we bumped fists and said, "Another one down!" We left the crowd, the bikes, the race announcer and the chaos behind. The northern side of Mt. Washington (trail north) would prove to be a most rigorous hike and yet, it was preferable to the spectacle of its summit.

We were closing in on Maine and Red and I needed to make a resupply trip before we continued. We left the trail at Pinkham Notch, about 40 miles south of Maine and decided to hike into Gorham, New Hampshire. "Sunflower" and "Gimme Shelter," two friends I made on the trail in Georgia, sent me a food box from Colorado and it was waiting for me at the post office. I had only hiked with them for a few days, but I was so out of shape I was slowing them down. Eventually, they pulled ahead, but we kept in touch exchanging texts, emails and phone calls. We remain close friends to this day.

The heat had soared like it often does in August, and the notch between Mt. Washington and Wildcat Mountain seemed to trap the humidity like a bath tub. Red and I were a little grouchy due to a navigational snafu. It seems we missed a turn and wasted a couple hours sightseeing. (Off-trail miles. . . grrr!) On the bright side, it could have been worse. I stopped to swim in a river and Red noticed no one was hiking past, which is when we realized we were lost.

When we finally made it to Pinkham Notch, we were hot, tired and frustrated. The little side trip wasted valuable town time; somewhere someone was eating the food we should've been eating. We crossed the road and stuck our thumbs out, that's when we met Paul from Montreal.

Paul was pulling into traffic in a white van trying desperately not to look our way. Our ragged appearance belied our friendly personalities, and he was doing his best to wait for a break in the traffic while escaping our pathetic pleas for a ride. His kind demeanor eventually won over, and he waived us across the street. When we opened the side doors to get in, Red and I hesitated. The van was immaculate. The white interior was clearly a product of obsessive compulsive disorder, complete with air freshener, fruit bowl and a basket of fresh vegetables. We didn't want to risk getting it dirty.

Paul from Montreal assured us it was okay, so we climbed in, cringing as chunks of mud from our boot treads broke free and scattered on the linoleum floor. As soon as the doors closed, the strong air conditioning quickly dispersed our body odor throughout the plush van, instantly making Red and I self-conscious. It was abundantly obvious that not only were we dipping below the socially acceptable hygiene level, so were our packs.

Paul from Montreal didn't seem to mind, instead of finding an excuse to drop us off at his first opportunity, he gave us a full tour of the town. When I asked where the library was, he showed us, and he eventually drove us to a popular Chinese Buffet. Red and I were so thankful for his hospitality that we insisted he join us, which he did.

Somewhere between our second and third trip to the buffet, Paul offered to pick us up the next day and bring us back to the trail. He was vacationing in the area and doing some hiking of his own. It was Sunday and we would have to wait until morning to go to the post office and library, so we rented a room at the motel adjacent to the Buffet. We spent the rest of the afternoon in the pool. We even washed our packs. After another trip to the Chinese Buffet and some ice cream from a touristy roadside stand, we repacked our clean, sun-dried backpacks and went to sleep in the air-conditioned room.

By the time the library opened, we had done our laundry, picked up my food box from the post office and had a big breakfast at the local breakfast restaurant. (We weren't back to traditional diners yet, but I wasn't complaining). As promised, Paul from Montreal was right on schedule and even took Red to Walmart while I used the library's computer. By 1 p.m. we were all heading back to Pinkham Notch in the clean white van.

We said good-bye to our new friend, Paul from Montreal, dubbed him "Trail Angel of the Month," and parted ways. The temperature was in the high eighties and we wanted to get started on climbing Wildcat Mountain. (We heard from a SoBo it was bad.) Pinkham Notch Visitor's Center was busy and interesting. We took our time visiting with other hikers who were sorting food boxes of their own. Oriole from Baltimore (duh...), shared his Mom's home baked-cookies with us for the second time! The last time she sent cookies, we were with him in Vermont. "Thanks Oriole's Mom."

The climb was indeed "bad." If I had to climb this in Georgia, I would have quit. The steep jagged trail and hot summer weather demanded respect. Underestimating either would be disastrous. When we reached the summit, we climbed an observation platform with an unobscured panorama of Mt. Washington. We looked with a sense of satisfaction and accomplishment as the clouds brushed the top. We took some extra time soaking it in before climbing down; it felt like we were saying good-bye.

When we were about a half mile past the observation deck, Red and I decided to turn back. We hiked back up to the summit where we decided to watch the sun set on "The Big W." Red set his tent on the deck and I tied my tarp. It was August 17. We sat on the platform eating supper with the company of hundreds of gnats. Red escaped them by retreating into his tent. It had been a hot climb and Red was unusually quiet in his tent. I was deciding if I was going to disturb him or let him miss the amazing sunset when I heard him rustling inside.

The zipper to his tent announced his return, and when I looked over, he was standing with a birthday cake complete with burning candles. My eyes were filled with tears as he said, "Everyone should have a cake on his fiftieth birthday."

Whatever layers of "dirty onion" I had left, were peeled clean on that mountaintop. As the sun set on Mt. Washington, standing on an observation deck, I couldn't think of anything more to wish for, so I just blew the candles out. Then, Red and I ate the entire cake.

"Everyone should have a cake on his fiftieth birthday."

Red Hot walks into his home state.

21

Maine

The last 48 hours in New Hampshire was an emotional rollercoaster. The journey was far from over; Maine had 281 miles of trail and it was known to be the hardest state yet. I couldn't imagine how it could be worse than New Hampshire, but just stepping over the line, the last state line, was going to be monumental. Having Red Hot with me helped to keep me focused. If I let my mind go, my emotions would take over. It had been a long walk and I was tired.

Red was feeling it, too. The reality that we might see this to the end was beginning to set in. The day before we actually stepped into Maine, we stood on top of a mountain looking east. Everything we could see was Maine. Red began to cry.

We began to do the math. Until this point on the trail, Red and I never even mentioned a finish date; we didn't want to jinx it. My older son, Dylan, was waiting for a date to meet me in Monson. He was planning to join me for the last 100 miles. Just the thought of seeing him again was enough to make me cry. I think he was more

Spider webs of Maine

excited to meet Red; he had become quite a fan-favorite on my You-Tube channel!

We occupied the time with sporadic conversation while the 14th State waited our arrival. We both had a lot on our mind, each drifting off for our own reasons, and then we'd pick up with another topic, usually about food. Our conversation was interrupted when we noticed a guy walk out of the bushes. He looked like a day-hiker. His long pants and sleeves looked clean and bright, and his pack seemed more suitable for books rather than hiking gear. Red and I were hiking through a brushy mountaintop area with a narrow strip of solid rock under foot when we saw him. His presence in this remote area struck us as odd, so we checked him out.

"You guys wanna see a plane wreck?" Now he had our attention. His excitement was obvious as we approached. He didn't offer much of an explanation, and even vaguer directions, but here was another adventure dropped in our laps, so we headed into the forest.

"Follow the forest boundary to the stump, then turn left." We tried that. "Maybe we turn right?" Still no plane. "Let's try the other way." Nope. We couldn't find it. We were standing on the edge of the mountain and the last option was to go down. "You can go," said Red, "I'll wait here. If you find it, whistle." I hiked about 100 yards through the brush and I located the wreckage. To my amazement it was a huge plane! I whistled to Red and we yelled back and forth a few times before I convinced him to join me.

While I waited for Red, I stood looking at pieces of a DC-3 scattered throughout the woods. The fuselage, wings and landing gear looked so out of place in the forest. The devastated plane was a grim sight. Standing there in the middle of the pine trees, on the silent mountain, was a somber experience. I wouldn't learn the heroic details for a few days when Red researched it, so we explored the site with muted curiosity before returning to the trail.

On November 30, 1954, Northeast Airlines flight 792 crashed during winter conditions with seven people on board. Although they all survived the crash, two died before rescue arrived. The pilot's decision to pull the nose up forcing a belly landing, as well as cutting all electric power to avoid an explosion is credited for saving the lives of those on board.

After seeing the wrecked plane, our mood turned. Our normal high energy, "ultra-fun" attitude had become reserved. The reality of stepping into Maine was about to happen, and deep down, neither of us believed we'd make it that far. Red was about to walk back to his home state, which he had dreamed about for decades, and I didn't want to water down the moment with light conversation. I hiked ahead of him giving him space.

When I arrived at the border, I removed my pack, sat on a log and let it sink in. I got a weak signal, so I caught up on my messages while I waited for Red. Within 15 minutes I heard Red's poles as he came through the woods. When I saw him, he was crying. He slowed to a stop in front of the sign, rested his forehead on it, and sobbed. The tears he had been fighting for days were released. He was back on home soil.

The trail was ridiculously wild in Maine. Giant boulders, frozen in time from millennia past, required climbing rather than hiking, especially in Mahoosuc Notch. Red and I had the privilege of passing through this area dubbed "The Hardest Mile" in the rain. It took us over an hour. When we finished the notoriously difficult section, we met a SoBo filtering water and stopped to chat.

When she asked us how "the mile" was, Red replied, "I'm glad it's over." Without missing a breath, she said, "Now you have 'The Arm' to worry about." In true SoBo fashion, she was referring to another rigorous section that lay ahead. Disgusted, Red walked away without another word.

When we finished the brutal climb, Red faced the valley and yelled obscenities to every SoBo who warned of the perils awaiting him. Although none of them would hear his rant, he felt better. Despite all their warnings, we were still moving north and nothing had stopped us yet. We were going all the way and we knew it.

The mountains of western Maine were as beautiful as any we had traversed thus far. The green trees and shimmering lakes carpeted the land with little, if any, signs of human activity. Occasionally, a trail of dust could be seen from a logging truck traveling an unseen dirt road, but from our vantage high above, it was easy to imagine an unexplored wilderness.

Red and I were hiking through one of these long stretches where the only traffic consisted of NoBos. The section-hikers were few, opting for the more accessible sections or areas with dramatic mountains. The dense forest was a tangle of damaged trees from the previous winter. The dead pines filled the air with the familiar aroma of Christmas, mixed with the smell of fresh sawdust from the trail crews. The trail sawyers cut a narrow path through the destruction; the bent birch trees with their white bark stood out boldly in the dark woods.

Other than the forest ruination, there was nothing to see. There were no clear lakes, scenic rivers or rocky outlooks. The brush hugged the trail and visibility was limited; it was an unlikely place for a reunion. When the trail led us down a small hill, we saw a group of hikers. As we approached, we were pleased to find some old friends. Five months ago, none of us had met. Since starting in Georgia, we'd gotten to know one another, and friendships were made.

Philco and All The Way from Tennessee, Papa Al from Wisconsin, Walnut from Georgia, and Happy from New Zealand, had just converged together as Red Hot and I joined them. We all started alone nearly 2,000 miles south, within days of one another. Somehow we all found ourselves in a thick patch of woods, on a narrow strip of trail, in the last state of our journey. There wasn't even enough room on the trail to stop. Most of us stood in the leafy vegetation.

We were two hundred miles or so away from beating the odds. I was the youngest at 50 years old, and Papa Al was the oldest at 69! We had out-hiked a lot of younger, healthier hikers, which made us a proud group. Our bodies were beat up and we were ready to finish, but not one of us was ready to quit. We decided to hike to the next lean-to where we took a long lunch break; after all, they were old.

Before we broke up to continue our own hike, Papa Al imparted this to those watching my videos from home: "You are only young once, how long your once is, depends on you."

"Loner"

"The only thing that could make my hike better is if I met Loner." Prior to leaving Connecticut, in order to prepare, I watched YouTube videos by a hiker in 2012: Loner (Loner2012AT). Red was Loner's biggest fan. We often referred to his videos as we hiked. Loner's down to earth attitude, simplistic approach to the trail and genuine kind

Loner meets us in Maine.

personality won us over from his first video. After the birthday cake gesture, I wanted to try to make Red's journey "even better," so I contacted Loner by email.

Months earlier I was honored to learn he had been watching my videos and was thrilled when he posted words of encouragement throughout my trip. He regularly mentioned Red Hot when he posted, so I thought it was worth a shot. He explained that he was living in North Carolina but he'd let me know if he headed north during the summer. While I was waiting for Red at the Maine border, I checked my emails and there was a notification from Loner! He was heading to Maine and if we were in the Rangeley area, we could find him there!

It was still 60 miles away, but if we pushed, it was makeable. The hard part was pushing Red without telling him why. I told him we needed to go into town to post a video, and hired a shuttle to pick us up at the trailhead. We actually had to run the last point-8 to meet our pick-up in time to avoid hitching nine miles to town.

When we got to town we went to The Farmhouse Inn. We took showers, tossed our dirty clothes in line to be washed and headed out to meet Loner – under the guise of going out for a hot meal. When Red was in the shower I told the Inn owner of Red's surprise, and she agreed to drop us off at Loner's motel. I had all the info in my phone.

We went into the lounge adjacent to the motel and we sat with IceMan and Mrs. IceMan. Red and I ordered beer while we watched them eat a delicious-looking pork chop meal. I excused myself to use the bathroom, but really, I went to Room 17 where Loner was staying. Unfortunately, the room had a "do not disturb" sign on his door. Remembering his email, and in an attempt to surprise Red, I knocked anyway. The very unhappy traveler staying in that room was pissed! I admitted that I had, indeed, seen the sign, apologized and inquired at the lobby desk. Maybe I went to the wrong room?

The manager was expecting me, having received a call from Room 17. He informed me that my friend wasn't a guest of his. I couldn't understand the mix up, and my phone was back at the Inn. I blew it.

To make matters worse, I couldn't stand watching Mr. and Mrs. Ice-Man eating the thick pork chops any longer so I ordered two plates, one for Red, and one for me; the moment of weakness cost me almost 100 bucks! IceMan brought us back to the inn and when I checked my email, I saw the problem immediately: we went to the wrong motel. Obviously.

In the morning, I tried again. This time I told Red we were stopping at another motel to meet up with some other hikers for breakfast. When Loner answered the door, Red was speechless. Hearing his familiar southern accent and seeing him in person felt like we were meeting an old friend. Over the next 48 hours we got to spend time with our trail mentor. We had a big breakfast, courtesy of Loner, spent time in town together, then hiked and camped on the trail. Red talked about it all the way to Katahdin!

When I first reached out to Loner, I thought he lived in Vermont, relatively close to the trail. When he went out of his way to visit us from North Carolina, we were moved. He really did make Red's hike better. Mine, too.

Dylan

Of all the miles I remember on the trail, number 1,988 stands out as one of the most difficult. Red and I were resting on the summit of Spaulding Mountain, checking our messages, when I received an email from my son Dylan. His travel from Louisiana placed him in Monson, Maine, three days ahead of schedule, and he was forced to head back four days earlier than expected. In order to meet him when he arrived, I had to go 86 miles in the next three and a half days.

I didn't say anything to Red Hot, but the change of plans would mean we couldn't summit together. We had made plans to meet his family at Baxter State Park and summit as a group, the change in plans meant I wouldn't be in the group. We hiked another eight miles that afternoon before stopping to camp. I had a pit in my stomach all afternoon, I had to leave Red behind and try to hike the remaining 78 miles in the next three days.

When I told him I wouldn't be camping with him, he was confused. I explained my situation and of course, he wanted to make the run with me. I was adamant, explaining that I would be hiking at night for the next few days and I didn't want him to risk an injury. Over the last two months, Red and I had become "sole brothers." Leaving him on North Crocker Mountain was the single hardest moment I experienced on the trail.

My head lamp exposed the few feet of trail as I pushed past the 2,000 Mile Marker, a landmark that otherwise would've elicited high-fives, pictures and trailside whoops. I hiked past with nary a glance. My next order of business was to get to Stratton, Maine, five miles from the trail, for supplies. Red and I had timed the stop for the following day, but I couldn't wait.

Luckily, there was a section-hiker sleeping at the trailhead. He watched me trying to hitch in the dark for a half hour and then waived me over. He drove me to the only place that was open at 10 p.m.: a gas station. I bought three days of energy bars, a plastic jar of peanut butter, a can of pie filling (they didn't have jelly), some peanut M&Ms, a dozen powdered doughnuts and a liter of Dr. Pepper. That, and the tortillas I had in my pack, was going to fuel me for the next three days. I stripped all the extra wrappers, placing the power bars in one Ziploc, the blueberry filling into another and M&Ms into another. The 12 individually wrapped doughnuts were stripped of the plastic and placed into the plastic grocery bag from the store. I threw my water bottle away, replacing it with the full Dr. Pepper bottle, removed the tamper-proof sealed paper from the top of the peanut butter, and threw all the garbage in the trash.

The Section-Hiker/Trail Angel watched as I did this without a word. When I was done, he said something about re-doing his food bag. He brought me back to the trailhead where I thanked him profusely, at which he replied, "Thank you... for the lesson." I hiked for about a half hour, set up my hammock and sat on the ground where I ate every doughnut and drank all the Dr. Pepper.

One of the things that irritated me the most when talking to other hikers was hearing about how many miles they hiked. By now mileage was a state of mind. Our bodies could handle as many miles as the mind wanted. The next three days would prove it.

The first day was the longest. I began before light and traversed the entire Bigelow Mountain Range making it to Pierce Pond Lean-to at exactly 3 p.m. The Kennebec River was four miles further. If I didn't make it there by 4 p.m., the canoeist, who is an ATC employee, would be off-duty and I'd have to wait until 9 a.m. the next morning. I went for it. I made it with seconds to spare. I felt bad for Dave, the ferry driver, because he had already pulled his canoe up on the bank on the far side. I saw him look at me, check his watch, and drag it back to the water. "It was close," was the first thing Dave said as he paddled up to shore. I was his 26th hiker for the day. I placed my pack on the bottom of the canoe covering the white blaze painted there, put on a life jacket, and Dave handed me a paddle. It was my first big day, and by the time we reached the far shore I was exhausted. He wouldn't accept a tip so I bought a coke and a couple snickers bars from his wife who had a tailgate stand parked on the road.

I was making good time and the trail continued to deliver beautiful views, pristine lakes and abundant blueberries. I took short breaks to swim and eat berries, but my plan to get to Monson kept each stop short. That night I didn't even set up my hammock; I slept on the ground, fully clothed. The only thing I took out of my pack was my sleeping bag and pillow. When I woke to my alarm before dawn, I put my shoes back on, packed my bag and left with my head lamp lighting the way.

I stepped off the trail in Monson by 3 p.m. on the third day. Dylan wouldn't arrive until morning, I was ahead of schedule. I was picked up by Poet and Hippy Chick, the owners of Shaw's Hiker Hostel, where Dylan was meeting me. I had become accustomed to sleeping outside, so Poet let me use his tent so I could be comfortable. I spent the rest of the day and most of the night reading a book; I was too excited to sleep.

Dylan showed up as planned. I'm not sure if the long hours of the trail had weakened my emotional state, or just seeing my son set me off, but I was overcome with emotion when he stepped out of the truck. Many miserable days were endured by looking forward to this day. He held me as long as I needed, just like I'd held him when he needed it when he was little. He had traveled 1,865 miles from Louisiana to finish my journey with me. I couldn't wait to show him my new world.

We spent most of the day packing and repacking, double checking his gear, visiting with others who were also staging for the last 100 miles of their hike, and several who had summited the previous day. When we were done, we were dropped off at the trail and hiked a few miles. We camped early making sure all his gear was up to snuff for the 100 mile wilderness. We enjoyed our first night of wilderness camping

without worrying about anything. We were just father and son, camping, laughing and telling stories. He spoke of his life in the USAF, and
I told him stories of the trail.

We were out of camp late... in hiker time. Yesterday, he had had a
long travel day, so I didn't have the heart to disturb him as he snored
away in his hammock twenty yards away; he was going to need his rest.
We managed to hit the trail by nine. When we arrived at the second
river crossing, about seven miles away, we both decided to jump in a
deep pool to cool off. The cold water felt great in the early September
heat.

When I was sitting on a rock putting my shoes on, I looked up and
saw Dylan running across the river and lunge into the faster current.
He reminded me of a bear chasing salmon. He had just walked out
of the river and I thought maybe he went in for one last dip. When
he emerged he was holding a sneaker in his hand! Another hiker had
dropped it in the river while crossing upstream. Dylan saw it and res-
cued the escaped shoe. I was proud of him, the natural reaction of a
father when his kid does something good. I was just glad he didn't get
pulled into the rapids! (Oops, there I go, acting like a parent again.)

The rest of the day was so fun! His enthusiasm to take in every
view, and his curiosity for what was around the next bend or over the
next mountain was contagious. We even climbed to the top of a fire
tower on Barren Mountain. The observation shack had blown off, but
we climbed up anyway and watched the sunset from high above the
trees.

I knew I'd have to cut my mileage back a little to keep him from
over doing it, but each time I suggested we stop, he'd refuse. He was
determined to make it to Katahdin before he had to go home. In all,
we ended up hiking too far on our first day. The last four miles wore
him out and his knee was bothering him. When we finally stopped to

My son Dylan joins me on the trail.

camp he told me he hurt it when he slipped on a rock running into the river.

It took most of the next day to travel 11 miles, and he was struggling with his knee, so we had to make a decision. I decided to carry his food bag to lighten his pack weight, and I took one of my knee braces off for him to wear, but it didn't help. His knee was swollen and I made the hard decision to take him off the trail. He was miserable, but I didn't want him to make matters worse by continuing on it. (He had responsibilities to Uncle Sam.)

When we hit the Katahdin Iron Works Road, we hitched out of the forest in the back of a pickup. They drove us to the closest town which was about 30 miles from the trail. From there, I called another friend named Paul. We met 25 years earlier, when we both stepped on academy grounds for our first day of training. After retiring, he moved to Maine. When I asked him for help to get our truck in Monson, he came to our rescue. 45 minutes later, we were back at Shaw's Hiker Hostel.

We slept at our camp that night which was in the area, and went to a diner for breakfast. Dylan still had plenty of time before he had to leave, so we stocked up on food, beer, soda and water, and then headed back to the trail to conduct trail magic. Even though he didn't get to hike, he got to meet the people I had come to know as my trail family. They all had stories to tell him, gladly accepted a beer or two, and thanked him for his service. He met the great people on the trail that I had been telling him about for months. It was a great day.

When he was asked why he was leaving the trail, he told everyone that he had to get back to work, instead of telling them about his knee. Dylan didn't want the news to reach the person who lost his shoe. He was afraid he would feel bad and with Katahdin looming; Dylan didn't want anyone feeling bad.

We camped in the woods near the trail. We hung our hammocks a few yards from each other and enjoyed our last few hours together. After a tailgate breakfast, he drove back to Connecticut, put my truck back in the garage and flew back to Louisiana. His time with me was the best four days I had on the trail. As I watched him drive away on the dusty logging road, it was the loneliest feeling I'd ever felt.

The last few days were an emotional rollercoaster. I pushed myself harder than I thought possible for three days, was overjoyed when Dylan joined me, then crestfallen when he had to stop. As I stood alone on the Katahdin Iron Works Road, the last thing I felt like doing was hiking the remaining 84 miles. I knew Red Hot was getting close. He had been 25 miles back when Dylan and I spent the day doing trail magic so I estimated him to be less than 10 now. I decided to hike on to try and shake my melancholy mood. I'd wait for Red when I felt better.

The Loneliest Day

It took me 17 miles. I hiked until I passed the last big mountain before Katahdin. I call it "the loneliest day." It was the rare day when I wanted solitude, and found it. It wasn't until late in the afternoon that I met up with Tortis from Texas. He and I hiked a couple miles before I left him to camp, and I hiked an additional five miles. They say you can see Katahdin from the summit of White Cap Mountain, and seeing it would have cheered me up, but the clouds were low and I didn't. Instead, I hiked down the other side for a mile and camped in an area that matched my mood: dark.

The clouds settled into the deep bowl in the mountains, and cold rain sprinkled while I set my hammock. It was a dreary site, but I decided to remain there in the morning until Red Hot arrived. I was around 71 miles from summiting Katahdin and I missed my buddy. I climbed into my hammock wondering how long I would have to wait.

I slept late, but due to the steep walls of rock and pine trees surrounding me, and the low overcast clouds, 8 a.m. seemed like 5 a.m. I left my hammock up with my guy-lines anchored to the middle of the trail with rocks, so Red couldn't miss me if he walked by. Then I went to the nearby lean-to and cooked some oatmeal.

By 9 a.m. Tortis arrived at the lean-to with good news: I won't have to wait long because Red Hot had camped with him last night and wasn't far behind! I was given explicit instructions to remain where I was, because Red had been trying to catch up for days... apparently there was a BOLO out on me (Be On Look Out). Tortis had breakfast with me while I waited. I was impressed that he had already hiked five miles, it was barely 9 a.m.!

We didn't wait long after all. Before I was done eating, Red came around the corner of the lean-to, threw his arms up and let out his signature, "HeyHeyHeeeey!" I was still bummed-out about Dylan, but I was happy to see Red. He had a big smile as he stood with his poles hanging from his raised arms, wearing his neckerchief and green hat. I jumped up and gave him a bug hug while Tortis stood laughing.

The next 40 miles blew by. The pull of Katahdin was stronger than ever, and we were right on schedule to arrive at the foot of the mountain when Red's wife and daughters arrived. Our combined excitement to complete the trail together propelled us through the woods like two deer running from a dog. The Hundred Mile Wilderness was full of unspoiled lakes and great camping sites. The sound of loons echoed through the night, singing us a final good-bye as we approached the end of our journey... it was almost magical.

The carpet of roots slowed our pace somewhat as we picked our way through the spaghetti-like maze, but our spirits were so high we didn't care. It felt like the trail was saying "We aren't done with you yet..." During the long tedious stretches, Red would look to the sky and yell, "Is this all you got?" His playful taunting was directed at an imagined control center responsible for dropping obstacles with a push of a button. We were getting more confident with every step. Our dream of becoming an actual thru-hiker was separated by one night on the trail... and one last mountain.

Before we entered Baxter State Park, where Katahdin is located, Red's wife met us and Red switched packs. It isn't uncommon; many hikers do that so they don't have to carry all their gear up Katahdin – it's a round trip. The pack he chose to carry was a relic. It was an old aluminum external-framed, bright orange nylon, retro model with hand sewn trail patches. I didn't say a word.

We hiked the remaining 10 miles through the park, finishing at the base of Katahdin. Tomorrow was summit day.

22

The Easiest Day

 Nearly six months after beginning in Georgia, Red Hot and I were standing on the gravel road leading to the summit. We were listening to three park rangers telling us that the trail was closed! Five miles separated us from transforming from long-distance backpackers to thru-hikers, and we were stopped dead in our tracks. The park limits the amount of hikers they allow on the mountain, and at 7:15 a.m. we arrived too late. Despite our personal connection to the trail, we were told that no exceptions would be made.

We were paralyzed. This day was such a focus in our lives for the last six months that it bordered on obsession. Red, his daughters Lily and Ali, his nephew Daniel, Red's wife, Renee, and I weren't allowed past a roadblock that was placed across the trail. The rangers, each with their park trucks, stood near the wooden portable roadblock... we weren't going up.

I attempted to speak with the ranger who seemed to be in charge, by asking if I could speak privately. "We can speak, but you still aren't going up," was his reply. We walked a few yards away from the other rangers, where I attempted to connect with him on a professional level. Honoring the foundation that binds all law enforcement agencies, he allowed us to pass. "Grab your things and go... I'll take care of those guys." The senior ranger winked as he nodded at the other two rangers.

His only condition was that we go without Red's family. Disappointed but not wanting to postpone our big day, they told us they would be waiting when we returned. We dashed past the rangers trying not to look their way; we didn't know when our luck would run out. We didn't slow until reaching Katahdin Stream Falls, about a mile away. With all the drama, we hadn't taken time to appreciate the enormity of this final hike. We sat near the waterfall savoring the sweet feeling of our upcoming completion. Tomorrow morning there would be no more miles to hike.

The weather was perfect: clear skies, cool air and a slight breeze. The previous day was a washout, resulting in the high numbers of hikers on the mountain ahead of us. We were the last hikers on the trail, however, so we were able to hike at our normal brisk pace, energized by the thoughts of seeing the summit sign. The smooth trail and professionally constructed steps took a drastic transformation just below the tree line, and slowed our progress to a crawl. In a short distance the gravel turned to stone and then the stone turned to boulders. The gentle incline quickly became steep, and with it came the smell of shampoo, laundry detergent and Axe Body Spray. We were catching up to the other 97% of Katahdin's visitors... the day-hikers.

Wearing the latest fashions ranging from Old Navy to Arc'teryx, the enthusiastic line of hikers pulled themselves over the boulders with their sweat-shirts and jackets tied tightly around their waists. They politely smiled with their rosy cheeks and let us pass. We commented to every Red Sox, Patriots and Bruins fan along the way, and jeered all others; after all, we were in New England.

Red and I seemed to be flying up the mountain. All the miles leading to this day had prepared us for this climb. Nearly five million steps had built our stamina, transformed our bodies, honed our coordination and ultimately made this the easiest day of the journey. Our jovial spirit launched us higher with every step. When we reached the tree-line we were surprised by what we saw... one long line of hikers!

The rangers were right, the mountain was full. There are a few areas where extra caution and effort is required, and these areas were bottlenecked. While we waited our turn to navigate the steel handholds, we enjoyed fun conversation with the friendly adventurers. Occasionally the group would shout encouragement to a struggling hiker, and then cheer as he or she conquered the obstacle. Red and I were having a blast.

Unlike most of the mountains we climbed, Katahdin was a jumble of boulders with very little vegetation on its steep side. This made it a little easier to climb for us, because we stepped a few feet from the trail and "used the fast lane." I'd look back every few minutes to check on Red and he'd be right at my heels, bright orange pack sticking out like a beacon.

With the last mile and a half remaining, we slowed to a crawl again. We fell in behind a long line of French-speaking Canadians. We communicated using the few French phrases we learned from our French-speaking grandparents, but "go collect the eggs" and "put wood in the stove" didn't seem to impress them. The mountain leveled off and the fragile vegetation was clearly marked, so we were forced to follow the slow group as we walked between rope barriers. One by one, the people we'd passed fell in behind us. After about a half hour the Canadians, with their Adidas sweat-suits and Member's Only jackets, stopped to take pictures, and we were free to hike the last mile at our own pace.

The reality of what we were doing had started sinking in and I was fighting to keep my emotions in check. Our conversation had stopped and we were once again lost in our own thoughts and feelings. The few times we looked at each other we were brought dangerously close to tears. With point-2 remaining, I suggested we take a break; I needed to pull myself together.

We could see the summit sign from the rock we sat on. The crowd of around 100 hikers took turns standing on it for pictures, and we could hear the occasional cheer. We knew it was going to be similar to our summit experience at Mt. Washington, so we let our emotions free and congratulated each other there. When we were ready, we'd hike the last few yards and take a picture, too. For now, we let it sink in.

During this journey, Red and I forged a friendship that we both knew would last forever. The trail is a long, hard test that pushed me much further than I thought possible. Having Red there pushing himself just as hard, helped me to find the mental strength to finish. Together we would tackle each day, regardless what lay ahead, with a positive attitude, unceasing energy and tons of good humor. We made a good team: "We're not Ultra-Light Backpackers. We're Ultra-Fun Backpackers!"

By now, my YouTube channel had been viewed over 100,000 times and Red was beloved by the viewers. In a world of mega online personalities that may not be impressive, but for a couple old guys, we were honored to have the small following. We wanted to express our thanks for the thousands of messages supporting us and to those who quietly watched. We shot a video and shared our gratitude and emotions with our viewers. I took this last chance to tell everyone Red's personal story, the one he told in Pennsylvania at the buffet:

"I've wanted to hike the AT since I was a boy. My father and I fished the streams along the trail in Maine every summer. When he told me that the trail went all the way to Georgia, I decided I would thru-hike it someday. I read every book I could find, researched maps and studied the trail for decades waiting for my chance.

"Baxter State Park and Katahdin were familiar to me as well, fueling my drive to hike the trail. Every autumn my Nanny (Grandma) would reserve a lean-to in the park and spend two weeks camping. She would pack her camping supplies in and spend her time hiking the trails and mountains within the park. She practically held celebrity status among the rangers and enjoyed visiting them at the ranger station. They offered to hike her supplies in for her, but she wouldn't impose on them. She would hike a 40-pound pack until she was nearly 80 years old! She would fill her orange nylon, aluminum external-frame backpack with trail patches on it and take as many trips as needed.

"I spent a weekend with her when I was a teenager, going up after school on Friday and returning on Sunday night. We hiked, camped, explored, fished and swam. She wasn't your typical Grandmother. Nanny tried to get me to climb Katahdin with her and I wouldn't do it. 'I'll climb it someday Nanny... at the end of my thru-hike.' She passed away 13 years ago and never got to see me summit. I sometimes regret not climbing it with her, it was her world and she wanted to share it with me."

When Nanny passed away, Red inherited a framed black and white picture of her sitting on the platform at the Russell Pond Lean-To, while the rangers visited her in the early '50s. The same pic-

ture can be viewed at the Baxter State Park Visitor's Center. It's his prized possession. He also inherited her orange backpack. The pack had accompanied her on several trips and had logged many miles on the park's trails. Red refurbished it. The frame was repaired, straps and zippers replaced, and patches resewn. For the last five years it held a prominent position on the wall of his office reminding him of the time spent together, and his close relationship he had with this special lady he called Nanny. He decided that when he hiked into Baxter State Park at the end of his thru-hike, it would be with Nanny's pack on his back.

"So as you can see, I've been planning this hike for almost 40 years." Holding the pack on his lap, and with tears in his eyes, he continued. "As far as I know, this pack never made it to the summit of this mountain, so today it will." Facing the heavens he showed her her own pack and said, "This is for you Nanny!"

By now we were both crying. We took another moment to gather ourselves and I said, "Are you ready to finish this up?" He nodded and we got up.

The last point-2 seemed longer than the entire climb. It seemed like I was hiking in slow motion. I knew Red was behind me, I didn't have to look. The crowd on the summit was loud and festive but I somehow blocked them out and focused on that sign, the symbol of an end to an amazing journey.

We approached the summit and stood, waiting for our turn to touch it. The day-hikers surrounding us could see our unembellished looks of calm, raw emotion and stepped aside. I stopped in front of the sign and waited for Red to join me. The sign was weathered and faded from the harsh mountaintop elements, but due to its signifi-

Red Hot with his Nanny's backpack

cance, looked completely different than when I stood here on my last trip.

Red's emotions could be held back no longer and when he stepped up, we touched the sign together. He leaned forward and rested his head on the sign fulfilling his 40-year dream. I stood beside him as he wept, proud to witness his transformation from long-distance backpacker to Thru-Hiker. Unable to speak, I tried to release my triumph with a whoop, but my choked throat and frazzled emotions failed me. I, too, had accomplished Thru-Hiker status. We unashamedly hugged each other on top of that mountain surrounded by strangers, just like the thru-hikers I met there a few years earlier.

"Now I see the secret of making the best person,
it is to grow in the open air
and to eat and sleep with the earth."
Walt Whitman

Afterword

When you turn away from the summit sign there are no trophies, no parade and no reporters. You just walk away. For the next five miles I climbed off the mountain knowing that tomorrow I wasn't hiking. It was over. Some continue long-distance backpacking. Not me. For me, that lifestyle I love is over for good. Sure, I could go hiking anytime but I knew it wouldn't be the same. Papa Al wouldn't be there complaining about how much water weighed. Easy Strider wouldn't be twirling his yo-yo and Red Hot wouldn't be click-clacking his poles – a sound I associated with having my close buddy nearby.

We spotted a few hikers in Millinocket on my way home but when we hit the interstate heading south, our umbilical cord was severed. The towns we passed no longer had the familiar faces we came to expect when we stopped. People no longer asked Red and I if we were thru-hikers. Instead, they looked at us in our hiking clothes and scruffy appearance, and looked away. Our normal fun chatter was hushed as Red's wife drove us further and further from the trail.

At Red's home in southern Maine, we parted ways with an emotional hug as flashbacks of hardships, laughter and poignant moments filled my head. As I drove off, this stranger-turned-friend, pointed and said, "I'll see you down the trail." It was his tagline, familiar to the thousands of viewers who followed us on YouTube. That friendship remains the most valued thing acquired from the trail.

Back in Connecticut, I did what most thru-hikers did: visited family, a few friends and ate... a lot. Most of them looked at me with concern due to my physical transformation and baggy clothes. I got a brief respite from real-world when I picked up Happy, a fellow hiker and friend who summited Katahdin on the following day as Red and I. He got a ride to Connecticut from Walnut, who was on his way back to Georgia. Happy stayed long enough for a shower, some pizza and a little sleep, before I drove him to Boston for his flight back to New Zealand. His visit was short, but his happy demeanor (hence his name) and our trail talk, kept me connected to the trail. When he stepped through the security gate at Logan International Airport my last remaining connection to the trail was gone.

The excitement of coming home soon faded and I found it difficult to sleep, opting for the couch. The walls in my empty house seemed to close in on me and I became depressed. My transition home was too abrupt. I was restless and I couldn't adjust, so I threw my pack in my truck and drove to the Green Mountains of Vermont.

The early fall weather was cool and the trees were just starting to turn, making it perfect for hiking. I found the trails easy and less traveled and I slept soundly in my hammock, but it lacked the AT feel. The people weren't there. Sitting in a fire tower with the cool breeze drying my sweat dampened shirt, I decided to try something else. I hiked out to my truck, drove back to Connecticut, grabbed my fly rods and waders, and drove five hours to Upstate New York.

In the past, standing in a river with a fly rod has been my cure for almost all ailments and attitude adjustments. After two weeks, however, I knew it was time to return home. As promised, my boss welcomed me back and within a few hours of returning from New York, I was turning wrenches. My brief celebrity in the garage quickly faded into the friendly banter I needed.

Working gave me the structure and routine I needed to adjust to the real world. Despite my healthy reintegration to society, however, I was a changed man. Similar to someone who has experienced a life changing event such as divorce, injury, service in the military or winning the lottery, my life is now split by a distinct event. Now it would be pre-hike and post-hike. Post-hike Sam didn't want to work in a garage for the rest of his life... He had a debt to pay.

I wanted to repay my boss for allowing me to leave for six months, so I worked for six months before turning in my resignation. During that time I found a way to stay connected to the trail. I regularly speak to groups around New England and bring the trail to them. I use this platform to be a good steward of the trail, teach "Leave No Trace" and share my story of renewed faith in people gained during my journey. My debt still loomed, so on the last day of work I loaded my truck and headed back to the trail.

The countless acts of kindness I received while on the trail had a profound impact on me. I felt like I was dunked into a giant washtub and cleaned from a career of negativity. Although I sent summit photos and notes thanking as many as I could, I couldn't possibly thank each person who picked me up hitchhiking, or offered me encouragement online and the people who offered me trail magic. So I decided to pay it forward. I drove south stopping at road crossings and trail heads offering trail magic to aspiring thru-hikers.

I brought coolers of drinks and bins of resupply. I drove hikers to town and back, camped with them, drove them to the grocery store, pharmacy and post office. By the time I was done, I had driven as far south as Sam's Gap in Tennessee and as far north as Katahdin. The leaves were changing in the 100-Mile Wilderness when my last fifty hikers were hiking their last forty miles toward Katahdin... with full bellies of giant hamburgers and Maine red-hotdogs.

I then packed all my belongings and moved to Maine. It was September and in an attempt of some sort of closure or something, I returned to Baxter State Park and climbed Katahdin again. I had driven thousands of miles, spent thousands and helped every hiker I could find... I was paid in full. In one last act of trail magic, I led two friends who I met a year earlier, Sun Flower and Gimme Shelter, from Katahdin to my new home, and welcomed them for their first post-trail night following their completion of the trail.

As for Red Hot, it turns out that his clients took to watching his hike on YouTube and he is somewhat of a celebrity now. His business is booming and Renee is happy to have him home. Our friendship, which was forged in the mountains and valleys of the Appalachians, will no doubt last our lifetime. We meet once a month at a diner, and spend an hour or so on the phone every Sunday night – talking trail, of course.

During my programs, people often ask me the same question: Did you learn any lessons? My lesson came in two parts: First, I felt like Superman for a while. The mountains weren't slowing me down, no weather was extreme enough and I had people from all around the world watching me; my head was getting too big. As I continued north, I watched Red fulfill his lifelong dream. He taught me what it meant to be humble, caring and a devoted friend. As I watched him, and how much his family meant to him, as well as how they all worked together to make his dream come true. I learned firsthand what a truly exceptional human being is. My change: Be more like Red.

The second part is more complicated.

Just before I left my home in Connecticut for the trail, in one of those half-hour visits in the grocery market aisle, I caught up with my longtime friend Penny. We could have gone on longer but we were shopping after all. She wished me luck on my hike and promised to follow along on YouTube and Facebook. I remember walking away thinking, "She deserves someone really great."

As fate would have it she found that special person. I watched on Facebook as she and her boyfriend shared their happiness with friends. When they became engaged, I reached out to Peter, Penny's fiancé. It was just a quick note introducing myself and congratulating them on their engagement. Not long after that I was excited when they eloped.

Sadly, Penny was killed in a motorcycle accident in September.

I had just made my way back to Connecticut and I was waiting in line at a Subway, when three burly firefighters walked in. He saw the last second recognition in my eyes and my too-late attempt to put my hand out to shake. Peter wrapped me in a tight hug and said through racks of tears, "I already know you. Penny and I watched every video together every Sunday night."

Now we were both crying. Everyone in Subway respectfully hushed, while Peter and I grieved for his wife, now only two days gone. I don't make many wishes, but I wished I could take his pain away at that moment.

My second trail related moment came around the same time: When the final video was published of summit day, hundreds of people from around the world contacted Red and I with congratulations. One message stood out from the rest:

"Thank you Sam and Red for allowing myself and everyone else to hike the trail with you through your eyes. What a beautiful experience! You really have no idea how much it means to me. I have been diagnosed with terminal cancer and given less than eleven months on this beautiful earth, so following you meant the world to me. Thank you, and Red, now I can leave this beautiful earth happy. God bless you. John"

My world stopped for a moment. I was overcome with emotion yet again. At that moment I reflected on how easily I could have walked off the trail: The knees; the poison ivy; boredom; my struggles in the beginning; and loneliness – each nudged me at different times. I am more thankful than ever that I didn't quit.

I tried to make contact with the author of that note, to no avail. I think often of those words and what they mean. I still can't recite them in front of the people attending my programs without fighting to keep my emotions in check. That note, which arrived weeks after my hike, made my accomplishment worth every step.

My biggest lesson is not profound. It is simply this: Try to be a good person, because you never know what kind of impact your actions will have on others.

About Sam Ducharme

Sam Ducharme returned to his home state of Connecticut following a year spent in Maine where he wrote this book. He continues to travel as a paid speaker, acting as a steward to the trail while allowing others to thru-hike through his presentations. His videos are available to watch free on YouTube by searching Sam Ducharme or Sam I Am Appalachian Trail. This is Sam's first book.

If you would like Sam to visit your school, library, club or corporation, contact him at samiam2189@gmail.com.

Or visit his website: samtalkstrail.com

For we need this thing wilderness
far more than it needs us.
Civilizations (like glaciers) come and go,
but the mountain and its forest
continue the course of creation's destiny.
And in this we mere humans
can take part – by fitting our civilization
to the mountain.

~ Benton MacKaye ~
Creator of the Appalachian Trail
1921